Sailing to the Holy Land

Crusader Ships, Seamanship, Logistics and Landing Operations

Dan Mirkin

BAR International Series 2904

2018

Published in 2018 by
BAR Publishing, Oxford

BAR International Series 2904

Sailing to the Holy Land

ISBN 978 1 4073 1659 8

© Dan Mirkin 2018

COVER IMAGE *Bohemond and Daimbert leaving the Levant (top) and arriving in Apulia.* History of Outremer, *William of Tyre, Book 11. Paris, BNF, MS Français 2628, Fol. 89v.*

The Author's moral rights under the 1988 UK Copyright,
Designs and Patents Act are hereby expressly asserted.

All rights reserved. No part of this work may be copied, reproduced, stored, sold, distributed, scanned, saved in any form of digital format or transmitted in any form digitally, without the written permission of the Publisher.

PUBLISHING

BAR titles are available from:

BAR Publishing
122 Banbury Rd, Oxford, OX2 7BP, UK
EMAIL   info@barpublishing.com
PHONE   +44 (0)1865 310431
FAX   +44 (0)1865 316916
www.barpublishing.com

To my friend and wife, Ronnie Mirkin

Acknowledgements

The present book developed from my PhD thesis, and I am deeply indebted to a large number of people and institutions for its completion.

I was guided gently but firmly by my supervisors, Prof. Oren Tal of the Department of Archaeology and Ancient Near East Cultures, Tel Aviv University, and the late Prof. Yaacov (Yak) Kahanov of the Department of Maritime Civilizations, University of Haifa. They saw me through the research project which was the basis of my thesis.

My study relies to a great extent on iconography, and many images had to be incorporated into the text. Numerous libraries, institutions and museums allowed me to publish images from manuscripts. Michal Semo Kovetz, of the Graphic Design Studio of Tel Aviv University, managed to sort out the chaos of text and visuals and convert them into a book. Carmela Karmi made the necessary drawings of images, such as mosaics, of which I did not have good photographs. The previous and present-day secretaries of the Chaim Rosenberg School of Jewish Studies: Sarah Vered and Liat Nissanov, guided me through the administrative intricacies. John Tresman's command of the English language improved the style of this book, and his knowledge of maritime matters informed its content.

The second part of my study deals with the problem of the maritime installation below Apollonia Castle: was it the port of Apollonia, or just a shallow mooring basin? The field research of this patch of water enclosed by sea walls required a great deal of assistance.

The Leon Recanati Institute for Maritime Studies generously agreed to help me in organizing the underwater research in the Apollonia 'Port', and lent me the necessary equipment, as well as the excellent services of Dr. Deborah (Debby) Cvikel, a very experienced leader of maritime research excavations, and the aid of the dive masters, Amir Yurman and Moshe (Moshiko) Bachar.

We could not have launched the research project without the help of Hagi Yohanan, the then Director of the Apollonia National Park, and no equipment could have reached the small area of sandy beach where we erected our camp without the help of the Reef Diving School of Herzliya, whose members daily performed impossible feats of small boat handling; threading their way through the surrounding rocks supplying equipment and other necessities to volunteers working in the 'Port'. My good friend Iftach Kuzik acted as executive officer for the field research conducted in the 'Port'. He managed to organize and obtain everything, be it sandwiches for the volunteers or pumps for water-jetting. Dozens of volunteers spent many hours under water in the 'Port', excavating, searching and photographing.

Dr. Hans Günter Martin (Abatanos) and Dr. Klaus Storch (Soso), conducted the preliminary underwater research with ground penetrating sonar, mounted on a rubber dinghy, ably assisted by Arie (Duba) Diamant, my sailing companion of many years. The results of this research permitted us to locate certain underwater finds.

Prof. Lorenzo Lazzarini of the Applied Petrography Department at the University IUAV of Venice analysed and identified samples of the columns found under water off Apollonia. This important contact was arranged by Dr. Carlo Beltrame, of Università Ca' Foscari Venezia. Omer Diamant free-dived to obtain these samples. Prof. Nili Lipschitz, identified the species of the wooden finds located under the seabed, which were later dated in a Swiss laboratory by 14C, some of them to the Crusader period.

Dr. Ehud (Udi) Galili kindly let me study and photograph the underwater finds he retrieved from the sea-bed near Apollonia; and Prof. Michal Artzy let me photograph and publish some of her underwater finds from Acre (Akko) port.

Last, but not least, I thank my wife, Dr. Ronnie Mirkin, to whom this work is dedicated. Her experience, knowledge and good counsel put the necessary wind in my sails while navigating through this endeavour.

Daniel Mirkin,

Tel Aviv-Yafo
August 2018

Contents

List of Figures vii

List of Tables x

Abstract xi

Introduction 1

PART 1: OF SHIPS, SEAMANSHIP AND FLEETS

Introduction to Part I 7

1 Types of Ships 8
The Ships of the Third Crusade 8
The Ships of the Fourth Crusade 9

2 Between Text and Images 10
Maritime Transport in the Crusader Period – Iconography and Rigs 10
Could Crusader Ships Sail Upwind?– The Peculiar Use of the Lateen Rig 10
Rudders and Manoeuvrability 17

3 A Modern Simulation of Richard the Lionheart's Passage from Acre to Jaffa 18
Why Was Richard Held up near Haifa? 19
Some Questions about King Richard's Timetable 20
The Simulation 20
Landing in Jaffa 21

4 Crusader Fleet Seamanship 23
Keeping Order 23
Skiffs and Other Small Boats 24
Small Boats in the Seventh Crusade 25
Naval Support of Land Operations 27
A Spectacular Naval Attack in the Fifth Crusade 30
Mooring, Anchoring Landing or Beaching 31

5 Ports of the Holy Land and Resulting Influence on Choice of Ships 32
Landing on the Coast of the Holy Land 32
Port of Acre (Akko) 32
Other Ports and Anchorages along the Coast 34
    Atlit 34
    Dor 34
    Caesarea 34
    Apollonia-Arsuf 34
    Jaffa 34
    Yavne Yam 34
    Ascalon 35
Landing on Beaches 35
Side (Quarter) or Stern Doors? 35
How to Get off the Beach 38

PART 2: APOLLONIA-ARSUF: A MARITIME INSTALLATION BELOW THE CASTLE

6 General Description and Research Project 43
- Apollonia-Arsuf in the Crusader Period 43
- Evidence of Use as a Maritime Installation in Crusader Times 44
- The Research Project 45
- Sub-bottom Sonar Scan 45
- Water-jetting 46
  - Water-jetting Attempt 1 46
  - Water-jetting Attempt 2 46
  - Water-jetting Attempt 3 47
- Significant ^{14}C Results 47
- The Excavation 48
  - Workforce 49
  - Tasks 49
  - Clearing the Seabed 49

7 Findings 51
- The Northern and Southern Walls (Breakwaters?) 51
  - The Western Seawall 52
  - Depths 53
- Entrances 53
  - Evidence of Sea Traffic near Apollonia-Arsuf 54
  - Did Apollonia-Arsuf Have a Port? 55

Final Thoughts 60

Glossary 61

Bibliography 62
- Works Cited – Primary Sources 62
- Works Cited – Secondary Sources 62
- General Bibliography 65

Appendix A: Sonar Investigation: The Harbour of Apollonia-Arsuf, Oct-Nov 2010 69

Appendix B: Positions of Targets Discovered by Sonar 87

Appendix C: List of Samples from Apollonia for Radiocarbon Dating Submitted to the AMS Lab (Institut für Teilchenphysik Eidgenössische Technische Hochschule Hönggerberg, CH-8093 Zürich, Switzerland) by Prof. Nili Liphschitz, Dan Mirkin and Prof. Oren Tal 88

Appendix D: Equipment Transported to Expedition Camp by Boat 89

Appendix E: Locations of Water-jetting in the 'Port' (redrawn by Ms. Michal Semo-Kovetz after original) 90

Appendix F: Original Underwater Drawing of the Western Part of the Northern Wall (J. B. Tresman) 92

Appendix G: Tide Table for 6 November 2013 93

Appendix H: GIS Representation of the Apollonia Installation 94

Appendix I: Excerpts from Ambroise – L'estoire de la Guerre Sainte, in Old French 95

List of Figures

Figure 1. *A fleet sailing to conquer Troy. Les Livres des Histoires du commencement du monde* (fourteenth century?) British Library, Stow 54, fol. 82v 2

Figure 2. *History of Outremer.* William of Tyre, Book 11. BnF, MS Français 2628, fol. 89v 11

Figure 3. *Louis IX sailing east. History of Outremer*, William of Tyre, Book 34. BnF, MS Français 2628, fol. 28v. 12

Figure 4. Vita of St. Mark: *The Voyage to Alexandria* (c. 1275). West Vault mosaic, Zen Chapel, San Marco 12

Figure 5. *Retour de Bohémond 1er en Italie.* BnF, MS Français 9084 12

Figure 6. Harbour scene – Kelenderis Mosaic 13

Figure 7a. *The Bayeux Tapestry* (detail) 13

Figure 7b. *The Bayeux Tapestry* (detail) 13

Figure 8. Lateen sail (Drawing after B. Landström, C. Karmi) 14

Figure 9. Detail of Richard de Fournival, *Bestiaire d'Amour*, MS M.459, fol. 22r, Pierpont Morgan Library 14

Figure 10. *Civitas Jerusalem* by Erhard Reuwich (detail) 14

Figure 11. *Arrivée de Louis IX à Nicosie.* BnF, MS Français 5716, fol. 40 15

Figure 12. *De Re Militari* Vegetius (c. 1270) Fitzwilliam Museum Library, MS Marlay Add. 1 fol. 86r 15

Figure 13(a) The Imperial fleet burns the ships of Thomas with Greek fire (thirteenth century?), from *The Illustrated Chronicle of Ioannes Skylitzes*, in Madrid (Figure 70) Biblioteca Nacional de España 15

Figure 13(b) Detail of *Homilies of Gregory of Nazianzus*, second half of eleventh century. Jerusalem, Patriarchal Library, Cod. Taphou 14, fol. 33r 15

Figure 14. Bohemund and Daimbert, Patriarch of Jerusalem, sailing for Apulia, in a ship flying the cross of St. George (c. 1232–1261), British Library, YT 12, fol. 58v 16

Figure 15. The King of France and his crusading army approaching a fortress manned by Saracens, British Library Royal 19 D. I fol. 187v 16

Figure 16. King Philippe Auguste awaiting his fleet. *Chroniques de France ou de St Denis*, British Library Royal, MS 16 G VI, fol. 373 16

Figure 17a. *St. Ursula teaches the Virgins to sail*, drawing C. Karmi, after Paolo da Venezia 17

Figure 17b. *St. Ursula giving instructions to her companions on the voyage to Cologne.* drawing C. Karmi, after Paolo da Venezia 17

Figure 18. Galley of Flanders under sail (1410) 17

Figure 19. King Richard's probable course from Acre to Haifa 19

Figure 20. Progress of author's passage simulating King Richard's passage from Acre to Jaffa 21

Figure 21. Progress of the author's passage simulating King Richard's passage from Acre to Jaffa with reference to winds (on marine chart) 21

Figure 22. *Departure of Ulysses*, Riccardiano 492, Publio Virgilio Marone, Bucolica, Georgica Anneis, Sec.XV, sesto decennio, Biblioteca Riccardiana, Firenze 26

Figure 23. *Débarquement de Hannibal en Afrique* (1493?). BnF, MS Français 366, fol. 114 26

Figure 24. *Siege of Orikos by Philippe of Macedonia* (1493?). BnF, MS Français 366, fol. 54v 26

Sailing to the Holy Land

Figure 25. *Le débarquement des Grecs à Troie* (1400?). BnF, Français 301, fol. 58v 27

Figure 26. *King Baldwin's battle in Ramla* (top), and *Approaching Jaffa* (bottom) (1474) BnF, MS Français 5594, fol. 109 27

Figure 27. Small boat helping to retrieve an anchor. Bodleian Library Auctarium MS D 4.17, fol. 1v 27

Figure 28. *Louis of France arriving in England*, from Matthew Paris OSB, *Chronica maiora II*. (Mid-thirteenth century), Parker Library, Corpus Christi College in Cambridge, MS 161 fol. 46v (new folio number f 50 v) 27

Figure 29. *Loading of St. Mark's relics in Alexandria*. Mosaic, Saint Clemente Chapel, San Marco (first half of twelfth century) 28

Figure 30. *Loading ships for the Crusade* (1352). BnF, MS Français 4724, fol. 6 28

Figure 31. Edward III sets sail to relieve Thouars. *Chroniques* Jean Froissart (1410). The Hague, KB, 72 A 25 fol. 349v 28

Figures 32–34. Three miniatures (early fifteenth century) British Library, Harley 4431, *The Book of the Queen*, fol. 196v 29

Figure 35. Crusaders attack Acre, Florence, Bibl. Medicea-Laurenziana, fol. 292r, Book 24, ch. 1 30

Figure 36. Siege of Damietta, 1248, Mathew Paris. *Chronica Maiora*, Parker Library, Corpus Christi College, Cambridge, fol. 59V, MS 16II 31

Figure 37. Acre, 4 January 1945. The right arrow points to the Tower of Flies; The left arrow points to the remnants of the watchtower 33

Figure 38. A – Seafront of the Pisan Quarter. B – Western basin. 1, 2 – supposed location of chains 33

Figure 39. Acre. A – Location of the thirteenth century wooden pier. B – Location of pier's wooden columns, C and D possible reconstructions of the wooden pier and of moorings 33

Figure 40a. The southern bay in Atlit and the Crusader mole 34

Figure 40b. Aerial view of Atlit bay 34

Figure 41. Crusader transport ship (detail), originally part of floor mosaic (1224). Displayed on wall, San Giovanni Evangelista, Ravenna 35

Figure 42. Longitudinal section of the *taride* built at Brindisi in 1278 for Charles I of Anjou, King of Sicily 38

Figure 43. *Arrivée de Louis IX à Limassol*. BnF MSS Français 2634, fol. 411 (c. 1310) 39

Figure 44. *Débarquement des Normands en France* (c. 1375). BnF, MS Français 2813, fol. 165 39

Figure 45. Crowning of Louis IV (left), assassination of Guillaume Longue Epée (right). BnF, MS Français 6465, fol. 159v (1455?) 40

Figure 46. The Naval Battle of Cadsand. BnF Français MS 2643 fol. 42v 40

Figure 47. Romance of Destruction of Troy (late fifteenth century). Bodleian Library Douce MS 353, fol. 31 40

Figure 48. Richard II meeting with rebels (fifteenth century). BnF, MS 2644, fol. 154v 40

Figure 49. Aerial view of the Apollonia-Arsuf port today 43

Figure 50. Remnants of the southern watchtower, 1953 (Central Zionist Archive) 43

Figure 51. GIS of part of the base of the northern watchtower and part of the northern wall 44

Figure 52. Remnants of the northern watchtower (Beginning to mid 20th Century – Central Zionist Archive) 44

Figure 53. Survey of Arsuf, PEF. Conder C.R., Kitchener H.H., 1882-1888 'Survey of Western Palestine, Memoir Vol. II – Samaria, Sheet X Section B. opp. p. 137' 44

List of Figures

Figure 54. 'Outer Area' 46

Figure 55. 'Inner Area' 46

Figure 56. Targets in the 'Inner Area' 46

Figure 57. Targets marked by yellow pins on Google Earth map. Green dot – piece of *Cedrus libani*;
red dot – olive pit; light blue dot near Apo 10 – metal-impregnated wood 47

Figure 58. The dredging pump mounted on the rubber dinghy, with a diving flag, moored in the port 48

Figure 59. Walking the boat in 48

Figure 60. Paddling out with empty air tanks 48

Figure 61. Diver clearing debris 49

Figure 62. Water-jetting 49

Figure 63. Water-jetting was carried out along the lines marked in red 50

Figure 64. Protruding ledge 51

Figure 65. Headers on a ramp 51

Figure 66. Western section of the northern wall (sketch) 51

Figure 67. Western section of the northern wall (photo) 51

Figure 68. Western section of the northern wall, from the north, with staircase-like ashlars 52

Figure 69. The trench at 1.2 m below water level 52

Figure 70. Headers on a ramp acting as foundation 52

Figure 71. 'Clean' stones recently uncovered 52

Figure 72. The shallow trench on the reef 53

Figure 73. Remnants of structure on the reef 53

Figure 74. Supply boat walked out after dismantling the camp 54

Figure 75. GIS map of the castle and outline of the installation completed 16 June 2014 54

Figure 76. Locations of ceramic and glass finds near Apollonia-Arsuf 54

Figure 77. Underwater assembly of ceramics – Acre port 54

Figure 78. Ceramic finds from Apollonia Castle 55

Figure 79. Piece of a column found under water near Apollonia-Arsuf 55

Figure 80. Thin section prepared by Prof. Lorenzo Lazzarini from sample of column 55

Figure 81. Section of PEF survey, Sheet 10, with the word 'HARBOUR' marked 56

List of Tables

Table 1: Percentages of prevailing winds in July and August, according to records for Haifa in 1937 (Sailing Directions for the Mediterranean, 243) 19

Table 2: Significant radiocarbon dating results from the 18 June water-jetting 47

Table 3: Underwater finds at Apollonia-Arsuf 57

Abstract

A great number of books and studies have been devoted to the Crusades and the Crusaders. Some works have discussed the religious aspects, some have studied the various Crusades as a social phenomenon, and others have endeavoured to describe these waves of knights, soldiers and simple followers through the eyes of Muslim observers. The First and the Second Crusades travelled overland, but it was eventually realized that maritime logistic support was of prime importance. The subsequent Crusades travelled mainly by sea, whether directly to the Holy Land, or first to Egypt, and some even to North Africa.

Many scholars have devoted their research to logistics and maritime aspects, such as sailing, water supply, and transportation of soldiers and horses; and their extensive research has resulted in a vast amount of information. However, there are questions relating to maritime aspects directly connected to this part of the world which may bear further investigation.

Part 1 of this book is devoted to some of these topics: which sailing rigs were used on Crusader ships, and what kind of ships – generally manned by Venetian, Pisan or Genoese seamen – were used in conveying forces to the Holy Land; how the fleets were managed; and how they navigated. It also examines how and where the Crusaders landed armies with horses in the Holy Land, and what were the connections between the coastal Crusader castles.

Most of the vessels of that era could not sail upwind. They could advance by sail only downwind, or at best with a beam wind, if the sea was not too rough. The usual rig of the sailing ship was the triangular lateen sail suspended from a long yard supported by a short mast. The lateen sail is rigged fore-and-aft, roughly parallel to the longitudinal axis of the ship. This work proposes that the Crusaders often used the lateen sail as if it were a square sail, rigged across the ship. This theory is supported by substantial iconographic evidence.

The castle and the maritime installation (port?) of Apollonia-Arsuf were found to be particularly intriguing, and became the subject of a special case study, presented in Part 2 of this book. Field research by the author consisted of two parts.

1) Emulating a sea passage of Richard the Lionheart; sailing from Acre to Jaffa, which proved the veracity of the descriptions of a similar passage made by Richard.

2) Underwater excavations by the University of Haifa, and sub-bottom sonar profiling by a team from abroad in the maritime installation of Apollonia and the sea around it. Finds from under the seabed, some radiocarbon-dated to the Middle Ages, may indicate sea traffic near Apollonia, and although the question of whether the installation was or was not a port remains unsettled, it seems that it was an anchorage for small vessels, rather than a real port.

The author has attempted to raise issues, such as where did the Crusaders come ashore in the Holy Land, and to advance some new propositions. He has also made use of his sailing experience of over 60 years, and local knowledge of the Mediterranean to investigate some of the problems that Crusader mariners may have faced; and has taken the liberty of disagreeing with some of the conclusions published by other researchers.

Introduction

Ignoranti quem portum petat, nullus suus ventus est[1]

I take the liberty of commencing this introduction on a personal note: I grew up on the shores of the Mediterranean and for the last 60 years I have sailed across it and along most of its shores, except, where, unfortunately, I was banned because of my Israeli citizenship. I have sailed in and out through the Straits of Gibraltar, the Pillars of Hercules and crossed the Atlantic in my yacht, sailed in the Pacific to and around Bora-Bora, cruised in Thailand, in the Andaman Sea, sailed in a replica of a Viking boat in the Baltic Sea, got caught in fishing nets near Tangier, and went deep-sea fishing on the Grand Banks of Newfoundland.

But for me, the Mediterranean – with its blue waters and fickle winds, the Aegean with its unpredictable, fierce Meltemi gusts, the Adriatic with its Bora, which starts without prior warning, the Gulf of Lyon with its Mistral, or the Levanter that blows through the Straits of Gibraltar – is the king of all seas. It is because I became familiar with the difficulties that can be encountered in all these seas that I became so intrigued by the Crusades: How did they manage their extraordinary acts of seamanship – transporting tens of thousands of people, equipment, pilgrims, knights and their horses in the small ships at their disposal? Some of these were sailing vessels; some were propelled by oars, dependent on manpower and, occasionally assisted by sails, none of which could advance against the wind for any substantial period of time.

In the lines below I shall try to raise some questions that, to the best of my knowledge have not been addressed to date in other scholarly works, or, at least, have not been fully addressed, and to advance some theories in response to these questions.

* * *

Sailing across the high seas, rather than along the coast, from the late twelfth century, shortened the trans-Mediterranean voyage (Jacoby et al. 2007b, 62), and this involved the question of navigation on the high seas, out of sight of land.[2] This merits separate research, and is not treated in detail in this work. Nevertheless, I will briefly describe the sea routes taken by the Crusaders, the fact that sailing also at night could not be avoided as related, for instance, by Ambroise in describing how Richard the Lionheart entered the sea, hoisted his sails to the wind and rushed during the night under the stars:

Qui encore crt mult deshetiez:
Entra en mer a lor congíez,
E fist al vent lever les veiiles,
E curut la-nuit as esteilles[3]
    (Ambroise 12288–12290)

The possibility that Crusader mariners made use of the recently introduced magnetic compass will be mentioned, and proposals will be made concerning possible methods of dead-reckoning navigation, and celestial navigation that may have been employed by the Crusaders.

* * *

In November 1095, Pope Urban II preached his historic sermon in Clermont, calling for an expedition to liberate Jerusalem from the yoke of the Saracens and to save the Christians in the East. Western Christendom immediately heeded the papal call and between 1096 and 1099, the first expeditions set out overland, via the Balkans and Anatolia, for the East. However, soon enough the need for naval support became apparent. The navies of the Italian maritime cities played an essential part in the support of the military operations for conquest of the Holy Land (Dotson, 2006, 64; Balard and Picard, 2014, 58). It was only by sea that forces could maintain contact with the West, receive logistical support, supplies, reinforcements and equipment and, at a later stage, horses and mounted knights. The Genoese, who arrived at Jaffa in June 1099 with a number of galleys, supplied the besiegers of Jerusalem with equipment and tools taken from their ships, as well as with timber (Asbridge 2012. 95; Balard and Picard 2014, 58; Grousset, vol. I, 1934, 215). They even supplied the Crusaders with food:

The ships, laden with food, put an end to their hunger
But could do nothing to extinguish their desperate thirst
(Sweetenham 2005, 198)[4]

The conquest of Haifa, Caesarea, Arsuf and Acre (Jacoby et al. 2007b, 58) could not have been achieved without the assistance of the Italian fleets, which were given many privileges in compensation, in some cases one-third of the conquered cities.

---

[1] 'If one does not know to what port one is steering, no wind is favourable' – Lucius Annaeus Seneca http://www.brainyquote.com/quotes/quotes/l/luciusanna100585.html

[2] Sailing across the open sea gains momentum at the 14th century (Gluzman 2010, 273, 276).

[3] Ambroise was probably a clerk, some say an itinerant musician. He was the chronicler of the Third Crusade, author of *L'Estoire de la Guerre Sainte*, which describes in rhyming Old French verse the adventures of Richard Coeur de Lion as a Crusader.
'…Took leave and lingering no more/ Boarded his ship and left the shore/with sails spread to the wind. That night/ He sailed having the stars for light.' (Translation: Merton Jerome Hubert)

[4] Quotation from Robert the Monk, *History of the First Crusade*, Book IX.

Sailing to the Holy Land

Once the coastal area was taken, the Italian vessels remained for surveillance and to help counteract the Egyptian fleet based in Ascalon until the conquest of that city in 1153.

While the first two Crusades chose the land routes as the main avenue of approach, and had to cross the Balkans and Anatolia, by the end of the twelfth century transport by sea was preferred not only for logistic support, but above all, for the passage to Outremer of major reinforcements. In 1191, during the Third Crusade, Philippe-Auguste approached Genoa to transport his troops, whereas Richard the Lionheart used the English *nefs,* cogs from northern Europe, the *busses* from Marseilles and the galleys of Genoa and Messina. In 1203 Venice built and armed approximately 230 vessels in order to fulfil its obligations under a contract concluded with the delegates of the Fourth Crusade. Frederic II used the naval resources of Puglia (Apulia) and Sicily for his expedition of 1227–1229. In 1247 Louis IX (Saint Louis) appointed two Genoese admirals to negotiate the charter of ships he required for his Egyptian Crusade. All these maritime projects enhanced ship-building in the maritime cities of Marseilles, Genoa, Venice and, to some extent, also Pisa. These activities and mass travel to Outremer generated profits for the maritime cities and to their ports, as well as to the ports of Puglia and Barcelona.

The requirements of the Crusades also generated new navigational techniques and new organization and management of the various fleets, which some scholars describe as a maritime revolution (Pryor, 2015).[5] Ships with greater carrying capacity began to be built in the second half of the twelfth century.

There has been much research into the Crusades, including the study of transport by sea of horses, pioneered by Pryor, and Dotson.[6] However, it seems that some questions concerning Crusader seamanship remain unanswered. For example, Ambroise and others describe how Richard the Lionheart attempted to to save the Christians from Saracen massacre by sailing from Haifa to Jaffa in only 12 hours. They even describe how he removed his leg armour and jumped into the water, which reached up to his belt (or groin, depending on the version). But how did Richard manage to sail from Haifa to Jaffa in about 12 hours? And where in Jaffa did he land? The beach is now, and probably was then, north of the port.

Among the questions research has not sufficiently answered is how horses and knights were landed from ships. Clari describes how the mounted knights descended from their ships during the invasion of Constantinople (Clari 1966, 68); but there is little information on how such landings took place in the Holy Land, and which ports, if any, were able to accommodate the huge Christian fleets. A theory is advanced in the present book.

Despite the extensive study of the port of Acre, it seems that some issues about that city have yet to be addressed. For example, how could such a small port accommodate a fleet of many dozens of galleys, assuming that each galley or 'round ship' measured over 30 m in length, and a fleet consisted of thirty to fifty galleys and round ships bringing the total length of the vessels to more than 1 km (even mooring ships side-by-side)?

The so-called 'Port of Apollonia' may have played an important role in establishing a connection between the Crusader castle and the sea, but what was that role, and was it indeed a port?

A substantial research project in and around the 'port' of Apollonia used boat-mounted, ground-penetrating sonar to locate underwater finds in its vicinity.

An additional underwater search involving more than 30 volunteer divers was carried out inside the 'port' itself.

Answers to some of these and other research questions can be found only by actual experience at sea. For example, I endeavoured to simulate King Richard's voyage from Acre to Jaffa in a yacht, during approximately the same dates and covering the same distances, solely under sail, in order to examine the veracity of the story, as told by Ambroise, at least in terms of the time Ambroise said it took.

I studied medieval texts and illuminations to understand the use of various rigs, modes of fleet operation and the use of small vessels. I tried to reach conclusions by studying medieval pictures and illuminations as, for example, Figure 1, that of a fleet sailing to conquer Troy:

Figure 1. *A fleet sailing to conquer Troy. Les Livres des Histoires du commencement du monde* **(fourteenth century?) British Library, Stow 54, fol. 82v**

---

[5] The beginning of this introduction is based on the chapter entitled *Les croisades et la mer* in Balard and Picard, 2014, 58–59.

[6] For example: J. E. Dotson, Ship Types and Fleet Composition, *Logistics of Warfare in the Age of the Crusades*, ed. J. H. Pryor, Aldershot, 2006, pp. 63–75, and J. H. Pryor, "Transportation of Horses by Sea during the Era of the Crusaders: Eighth century to 1285 A.D.", *Mariner's Mirror* 68.1, 1982, pp. 9–27. 68.2, 1982, pp. 103–126.

This painting has, obviously, nothing to do with Troy, and is the fruit of the imagination of the medieval artist. One should approach the medieval images contained in manuscripts or otherwise (for example in mosaics) with caution. However, the reservations as to the accuracy of the details in such images notwithstanding, one can learn a lot from any such image. From this particular one we could learn that the ships used to tow small boats, that they had stern rudders (as opposed to quarter rudders), and that they had square sails rather than lateen rigs.

I attempted to trace the use of floating sea anchors, or regular anchors meant to dig into the seabed in ancient writings. I found it astounding that the seamen, manning the ship in which the Apostle Paul was transported, to Italy, took action similar to that which modern sailors would take when facing the risk of running aground. Because they were afraid they would run aground on the sandbars of Syrtis, they lowered the sea anchor and let the ship be driven along. (*Acts* 27:17, New International Version).[7] On the other hand, when faced again with the danger of being smashed against the rocks, these ancient sailors preferred to anchor with the stern facing the elements, a choice that would seem strange to the modern skipper: 'And they took soundings and found *it* to be twenty fathoms; and when they had gone a little farther, they took soundings again and found *it* to be fifteen fathoms. Then, fearing lest we should run aground on the rocks, they dropped four anchors from the stern, and prayed for day to come.' (*Acts* 27:28). The episodes described in the Acts took place well before Crusader times, but they serve as examples of ancient seamanship, which developed slowly until it reached the sophisticated capabilities of the medieval seaman. The storms suffered by Apostle Paul were typical of the area, and may be similar to those that dispersed the fleet of Richard the Lionheart when he sailed to Cyprus.

It is known that medieval ships could not efficiently beat upwind. Actually, even modern sailing yachts cannot sail directly against the wind, but they can advance in the general direction against the wind by tacking. Medieval ships could only sail with the wind behind them or, in the best case, with the wind abeam. So how did they reach their destinations in the Mediterranean, where the winds are notoriously fickle?

How much could they advance by rowing? What kind of sails did they have? Did they use small boats for assisting them in their manoeuvres?

* * *

The three-pronged approach I have used, viz. studying primary literary and iconographic sources, secondary sources, and organizing field projects, resulted in the discussion of the following main topics, in two parts:

Part 1 deals with the following points:

- General discussion of seagoing vessels used by the Crusaders.
- Vessels of the Third and the Fourth Crusades.
- Study of iconographic sources reflecting various kinds of maritime transport, which also presents a theory concerning the use of the lateen rig, and use of small liaison boats.
- A sailing passage simulating descriptions from primary sources of Richard the Lionheart's passage from Acre to Jaffa.
- Crusader fleet seamanship and management. Naval support of land operations, landing and beaching techniques and their applicability to Holy Land ports

Part 2 is devoted to the maritime structure located at the foot of Apollonia-Arsuf Castle ArsufArsufIt ArsufArsufis the subject of the following studies:

- General description and photographs, including GIS scans and drawings.
- Sub-bottom profiling with ground penetrating sonar near the reefs surrounding the 'port'.
- Water-jetting targets located by the sonar, and sending finds for carbon 14 analysis. Underwater excavation in the 'port' by volunteer divers, clearing debris, measuring and drawing the structures.
- Studying two granite columns found underwater off the shore, and discussing petrographic analysis performed in Italy.

---

[7] Although in some versions, as, for example, in the New English Bible, they lowered the sail rather than a floating anchor: 'Then, because they were afraid of running on the shallows of Syrtis, they lowered the mainsail and let her drive.' in the French translation: '… dans la crainte de tomber sur la Syrte, on abaissa les voiles' (La Sainte Bible, Paris, 1954).

PART 1

OF SHIPS, SEAMANSHIP AND FLEETS

Introduction to Part I

One of the longest frontiers of the Holy Land is the coast. An efficient way to transport troops, provisions, horses and pilgrims from Europe to the Eastern Mediterranean was by sailing across the sea from any European port, be it Marseilles, Aigues Mortes, Sicily, or even Constantinople.

This became obvious even during the First Crusade, although most of its forces marched overland (Dotson in Pryor 2006, 64). It quickly became evident that any long-term Western presence on the Eastern shores of the Mediterranean would require reliable maritime supply (ibid.).

In modern times, ships are divided into three main categories: warships, cargo ships and passenger ships.[8] The fleets that transported the Crusaders were rather a mixed lot, relying mainly on ships supplied by the Italian maritime states. Some of the Crusaders came from countries that were not classically seafaring in nature, for instance, Germany. The Crusaders themselves were rarely seamen. It is actually a paradox that operations often grouped under the collective name 'Passage d'outre mer'[9] involved tens of thousands of landlubbers (Mollat 1967, 345; Rubenstein 2011, 55–79; William of Tyre, second book and many others). Some did not have the financial means to travel by sea. Some resented travelling over the water.

Nevertheless, over the years, a multitude of ships was used to ferry the Crusaders and those accompanying them. And, indeed, since the religious principles of the Crusaders obliged the knights to allow various crowds to accompany them, they had to travel in company with numerous pilgrims and penitents (Grousset 1934, vol. II, 223). Women also were not excluded. A slightly humorous note can be detected in the *Chanson d'Antioche*, a rhymed epic poem of the first Crusade describing how young virgins accompanied their fathers who caused them to be born.

> Beaucoup de dames prirent la croix
> Et les nobles pucelles que Dieu a bien aimées
> S'en furent avec les pères qui les ont engendrées'[10]
> (*Chanson d'Antioche*, 50)

We should therefore visualize a great mixture of ships, which necessarily sailed at different speeds, used different means of propulsion and defense, and possessed different capabilities of withstanding difficult seas and bad weather; all this combined with the inherent difficulty, not to say impossibility, of sailing upwind.

---

[8] Although World War I and II saw the introduction of 'Merchant Cruisers' – cargo ships equipped with guns for self-defense, and the East Indiamen were well known for being able to defend themselves (http://en.wikipedia.org/wiki/Armed_merchantman).
[9] Passage beyond the sea.

[10] Many ladies took the cross/ and the noble virgins who were beloved by the Lord/ went away with the fathers that created them.

Chapter 1

Types of Ships

Many sources refer to various ships used to transport troops, pilgrims,[11] (including women), luggage and horses: de Sandoli, 1978 II, XI, refers to the fast-running *dromons* which he describes as measuring 40 m long, 7 m wide and 5 m high, with 25 oars on each side and one or two masts, capable of carrying over 50 men and women with their luggage, and sporting two castles of wood on the bow and stern. De Sandoli also refers to a type of ship called a *buza* used for transportation, but the best known are the *galera*, *galea* or galley for fighting, which could also carry 157 fighting men besides horses, women and other staff., There were many other types of craft, such as the rostrate (a vessel with a beak-like projection from the bow used to ram enemy ships) the *gate* (also called *catte*), and the *gulafri*.[12] Another ship often referred to in various manuscripts is the *tarida* or *taride* – a shallow craft, propelled by oars and/or by sails on two masts, to which further reference is made below, used for transporting goods, troops and horses (Jabour 2012, 11).

Saewulf, a pilgrim who made his way to Jaffa in or about 1102, recounts his terrifying landing in the Holy Land, when about 30 ships anchored opposite Jaffa 'port' dragged their anchors in a storm[13] and were wrecked on the beach. Some of these ships, as he says 'are commonly called Dormundi, others Gulafri and others Catti' *(Saewulf* 1892, 8). The footnote to his tale qualifies the *dormundi* as similar to the *'dromones'* The *'catti,'* Saewulf states, 'were probably similar to the Norwegian *colliers*, having a narrow stern, projecting quarters, and a deep waist,' whereas the 'Gulafri' were probably some form of galley' (*Saewulf* 8, footnote 1). Rather similar remarks are made in a different version of Saewulf's story:

Thus of thirty ships of largest size, of which some were *dromonds* (that is to say, having two tiers of double oars), *gulafri* (a sort of galley) and *catts* (vessels narrowing at the stern, with overhanging quarters and a deep waist). (Boulting 2001, 81).

However, very large ships apparently came into service for transporting cargoes during the second half of the twelfth century, before the Third Crusade. This is illustrated in March 1173, when Romano Mairano, a Venetian merchant, undertook to transport 1,400 trunks from Verona, and 600 planks of fir from Venice to Alexandria, the weight of which may have reached 450 tons. Mairano operated a three-masted ship, probably one of the largest vessels sailing the Mediterranean at the time (Jacoby 2005, 110).[14]

The first two Crusades marched overland, while the Third Crusade was the first in which troops were carried overseas by ships. I therefore briefly discuss the composition of the fleets of the Third and Fourth Crusades. Relevant information on the Fifth and Sixth Crusades is also presented, for example, the naval operations for the attack on Damietta during the Fifth Crusade, as well as the special horse-carrying vessels of Louis IX in the Seventh Crusade.

The literature of the Sixth Crusade, also known as the Crusade of Frederic II, reveals no special phenomena relative to seamanship, over and above what was mentioned briefly in the Introduction. One noteworthy fact concerning the departure of the fleet in the summer of 1227, at Brindisi, the intense heat, the problem of potable water and disease struck down many of the Crusaders, so a good portion of the army returned home. Also significant is that the Emperor himself did not depart (Madden 2006, 158). He landed in Acre only on 7 September 1228 (Mayer 1991, 235), and finally managed to regain control of Jerusalem.

The Ships of the Third Crusade

Three fleets transported participants in the Third Crusade to the Holy Land: one of King Richard the Lionheart, one of the King of France, Philippe Auguste, and the third, from northern Europe, sailed by Danes and Frisians. The latter fleet consisted of 50 cogs carrying 12,000 armed warriors, which arrived in time to assist the forces attacking Acre, but then found themselves surrounded by the Turks (Nicholson 1997, 71–72). The cog was a typical northern European ship, probably with straight stem and stern, with a deep draught which allowed it to sail better than flat-bottomed ships (Landström 1969, 77).

The two other fleets, of Richard and Philippe Auguste, started their passage from Messina. After its arrival in Messina, King Richard's apparently magnificent fleet was described as 'la merveille des enekes'[15] (Ambroise 535). Richard's war

---

[11] The term *peregrini* covered both pilgrims and Crusaders, as is seen for instance, with respect to the passengers of the ship *St Victor* in 1250. Occasionally, though, the former were distinguished from the latter, called *milites peregrini* or *peregrini crucesignati*. *Peregrini* sailing with their horses were obviously Crusaders. (Jacoby 2007b 58–59).

[12] This probably refers to various kinds of boats, as described in *Saewulf*, 26

"...miserunt quamplures perierunt perpauci quippè proprià virtute confidentes ad litus illesi pervenerunt Igitur ex navibus tri ginta maximis quarum quaedam dormundi quaedam vero gulafri quaedam autem catti vulgariter vocantur omnibus oneratis palma riis vel mercimoniis antequàm a litore discessissem vix septem il lesae permanserunt Homines verô diversi sexûs plusquàm mille die illâ perierunt majorem etenim miseriam unâ die nullus vidit ocu lus sed ab his omnibus suî gratiâ eripuit me Dominus cui honor et gloria per infini ta secula amen."

[13] A ship drags its anchor if the pressure of the wind and/or the waves is so strong that the anchor loses its grip and is pulled out from the seabed.

[14] Although apparently, Muslim ships of the eleventh century and first half of the twelfth century were generally larger and could carry several hundred passengers, there is no evidence of Christian ships of corresponding size (Jacoby 2008, 82).

[15] Probably meant to be *sneckas* (Nicholson, 1997, 174), the *snecka* or the *knorr* being a long narrow boat associated with the Vikings.

horses were apparently transported to Messia in *dromons*, as Ambroise described: 'Issi vint li reis el rivage/Si ot encontre lui son barnage/Ses biaus destriers lui amenerent/ Qui en ses dromonz venu erent.' (Ambroise 595)[16]

In Messina Richard the Lionheart met Philippe Auguste. They wintered in Messina and the French king set out directly for Acre on 30 March 1191. However, King Richard was not yet ready:

> Li reis Richarz ne pot movoir
> Kari l n'ot prest son estoveir,
> Ses gales ne ses uissiers
> A porter ses coranz destriers
> E s'armeure e sa vitaille.
> (Ambroise 1025–1030)[17]

Richard had also been waiting for his future wife Berengaria (Nicholson 1997, 174). He finally set out 17 days after the French king.[18]

These few lines by Ambroise reveal a great deal of information about Richard's fleet: It has galleys, and horse-carrying vessels (*uissiers)*. The fleet also had at least one ship known as a *buss*, a large transport ship, since Queens Joanna and Berengaria arrived at Limassol aboard a *buss* (Nicholson 1997, 178). It appears from various sources that King Richard's fleet contained between 39 and 52 galleys (Pryor forthcoming, and sources therein, 8).

We do not know the exact composition of the French King's fleet, but, apparently, part of it consisted of *busses* – (Nicholson 1997, 177). From 1189 to 1190 Philippe Auguste appointed the noble Hugues III of Burgundy to negotiate with Genoa for the supply of transports for 650 knights, 1,300 squires (*écuyers*) and 1,360 horses (Sivéry 1993, 105). A fourteenth-century miniature[19] that depicts King Philippe Auguste awaiting his fleet, shows rather large, two-masted ships.

The Ships of the Fourth Crusade

The appendix to Clari's *Conquest of Constantinople* entitled 'Note on the Fleet and the Forces' reads as follows:

> Contemporary accounts of the expedition generally agree in describing the fleet as made up of three types of vessels: galleys (galee, galiae), 'ships' (nes, naves), and horse transports (uissiers, usariae). The galleys were the fighting convoys, long narrow vessels propelled by oars, with auxiliary sails. The galley of this time was about 100 feet overall, and it carried a crew, mariners and rowers, of more than 100, and a certain number of marines, largely archers and crossbowmen. The ships were the large merchant vessels or freighters, converted into transports. They were sailing vessels, usually two-masters and two-deckers, broad in the beam and capable, some of them, of carrying a thousand passengers or more.... We need not suppose that all the transports supplied by the Venetians were as large as this. Probably there were only a few of these great ships, built especially for the leaders....the *Aquilla* mentioned by Danulo....there were only four or five ships in the fleet that were high enough to reach the wooden towers which the Greeks built on the walls.[20] The horse transports, or uissiers (so called from the huis or door in the side), belonged, it seems, to the general type of the galley; they were long narrow vessels propelled by oars, with space in the shallow hold for a number of horses. Jal reckons that the uissier of this time carried about 40 horses and 80 squires, in addition to the crew. (Clari 1996, 132)[21]

Jal, however, speaks about different kinds of horse transports (*usiae, ussaria, usserius, user, huisserius*) (Jal 1840, 429), He quotes Joinville, who explains how after the horses were placed on board the gate or door at the stern had to be waterproofed 'like a barrel.' In Joinville's Old French:

> Acelle journee que nous entrames en nos nez fist l'en ouvrir porte de la nef et mist l'en touz nos chevaus ens que nous devions mener outré mer, et puis reclost l'en porte et l'enboucha l'en bien aussi comme l'en naye un tonnel. (Joinville 220)[22]

Jal also distinguishes between horse-carrying vessels propelled by oars, and round ships propelled by sails only, which needed tugs (*remorques*), probably in order to facilitate manoeuvring, especially when landing horses (Jal 1840, 431). With regard to the size of the horse-carrying vessels, Jal thinks that the horse-carrying transports chartered by Louis IX from the Venetians (in the Seventh Crusade) could carry 50 horses each[23].

The use of the horse-carrying ships with an opening door that becomes a bridge (most probably in the stern, as discussed below) is documented by Clari, who describes the first landing of the Venetian forces near Constantinople:

> As soon as they had made land (the ships carrying the knights), the knights issued forth from the transports on their horses; for the transports were made in such a way that there was a door that could be opened and a bridge thrust out by which the knights could come out and land all mounted. (Clari 1966, 68)

---

[16] 'When the king's ship approached the bank/His barons and his knights of rank/Met him and led his steeds of war/Which transport-ships had brought before.' (Translation: Merton Jerome Hubert)
[17] 'King Richard cannot move from there/ for still unready is his gear/ The ships and galleys that he needs/ For transport of his battle steeds,/ His armor and supplies as well.' (Translation: Merton Jerome Hubert).
[18] The exact date of Richard's departure is not clear. Ambroise simply says that he set out on Wednesday of Holy Week, for the glory of God. 'Co fud la semaine penose…Al sucurs Deu e a sa gloire. Le mescredi de la semaine' (Ambroise 1186). This may not necessarily be correct.
[19] See below, Fig. 16.

[20] Of Constantinople.
[21] De Clari refers to Archéologie Navale of Jal, vol. 1 p. 480. I did not find it on this page, but rather, various references to *huissiers*, which he spells with an initial H.
[22] 'On that day, when we have entered our ships, the door of the ship was opened and all the horses that we had to carry beyond the sea [*outre mer*] were put on board. Then the door was closed and sealed as one would seal a barrel.'
[23] Each horse was accompanied by two squires and one knight, in addition to the mariners, crew, etc.

Chapter 2

Between Text and Images

Maritime Transport in the Crusader Period – Iconography and Rigs

Pictorial evidence is one of the sources that may help us in our attempt to understand, reconstruct, or at least to try to imagine, the shape, structure and functioning of ships and boats used by the Crusaders. While proportions are often distorted, it seems that the description of the rigs is significant, and leads to conclusions concerning the shape of sails and the manner in which they were used. However, before proceeding, some attention should be paid to the problems and risks inherent in using iconography as a direct source of information. Illuminations, obviously, are not, and never were, an exact reproduction of reality, and, as aptly put by Burningham and de Jong:

> However, these artists obviously satisfied their audience. The ships they drew must have been recognized as representing .... ships of the time. As with caricatures, many relative dimensions will be accurately represented even though the overall form is distorted. (Burningham and de Jong 1997, 288)

Flatman argues 'Manuscript illuminations provide detailed and often relatively accurate depictions of crafts like shipbuilding, structures like wharves and revetments, and activities like rowing, sailing and steering.' (Flatman 2004, 1276)

Thus, some of the texts quoted below may be considered confirmed by many of the illustrations that follow. According to Lillian Ray Martin the majority of medieval Mediterranean ships had lateen rigs (Martin 2001, 141)[24]. Before the advent of this sail most sailing vessels were square-rigged. There are many theories as to the origin of the lateen sail in the Mediterranean. Lateen-rigged vessels sailed in the Pacific Ocean as well, where this rig probably developed independently. As for the Mediterranean, most researchers think that the lateen-rigged vessels that navigated it developed in the Indian Ocean (Campbell 1995, 4). The lateen sail is widely regarded as the sail of Arab seafarers, and some scholars attribute its diffusion to the expansionism of Arab sailors (Campbell 1995, 4). However, based on further research, Campbell argues that the lateen sail developed in the Mediterranean and in the Indian Ocean independently:

It seems, therefore, that there is no longer a basis for deriving the European fore-and-aft sail from the Arab expansion into the Mediterranean Sea. The fact is that both in the Mediterranean and the Indian Ocean, the Arabs learned the use of the lateen sails from those who were on the sea before them (Campbell 1995, 12)

In his foreword to Martin's book[25], Marco Bonino explains that our knowledge of ancient[26] ships in the Mediterranean region resulting from archaeological sources has advanced in recent years more than our knowledge of ships and shipping of the Middle Ages in that region. Hence the importance of evidence from complementary sources, literary as well as iconographic.

In this section I shall try to analyse iconographic evidence, and, where possible, compare the pictorial evidence with the relevant sections in a contemporary medieval texts, such as that of William of Tyre *A History of Deeds Done Beyond the Sea*, otherwise known as *History of Outremer*.[27]

Could Crusader Ships Sail Upwind?– The Peculiar Use of the Lateen Rig

In order to be able to sail upwind efficiently, which means sailing with the bow of the ship at an angle of less than 90 degrees to the wind, the ship needs two prerequisites: a relatively aerodynamic sail plan, and an underwater configuration that provides some kind of lateral resistance, such as a keel or, at least, a deep enough draught. Failing this, even if the ship manages to claw its way upwind, it will be pushed sidewise, or, in other words, incur leeway[28] that would cancel out, or nearly cancel out any forward progress. This would become even more dramatic when trying to make way against waves. Most Crusader ships, whether round ships or galleys, did not have a deep draught. My contention is that, due to their hull shape, medieval ships could not make any substantial way against the wind, if at all. So, assuming that the lateen sail could theoretically enhance the upwind performance of a vessel, due to its aerodynamic qualities, it would be of no avail to the medieval ship, which would make excessive leeway[29] because of its lack of lateral

---

[24] A lateen rig consists of a triangular sail hung off a long inclined yard supported by a relatively short mast, and it is essentially a fore-and-aft sail, rigged in a manner parallel to the axis of the ship (see Figures 10a and 10b). 'The lateen rig is one of great antiquity, believed to be pre-Christian, and probably of Arab origin.' (Kemp 1976, 466) The yard was formed of two or more pieces bound together, and in a great vessel may weigh more than a ton).

[25] Martin 2001, Foreword.
[26] That is, before or in the first centuries of the Christian Era.
[27] Hereafter, in the present chapter, referred to as *History*.
[28] 'Leeway' means sidewise movement of the ship due to the pressure of the wind on the sail, and, to some extent also due to the action of the waves, when trying to sail upwind. Kemp (1976, 474) defines leeway as 'The distance a ship is set down to leeward of her course by the action of wind or tide'.

When Ibn Jubayr sailed from Acre to Cartagena, when beating upwind he advanced at 85 degrees over the ground, which means that his progress was no more than 5 degrees upwind. (Kahanov and Jabour 2010, 85).
[29] Some researchers cast doubt on the degree of superiority of the lateen rig over the ancient square rig (Pryor 1988, 33). Others concluded that there is virtually no difference in the potential performance of the square rig and the lateen-rigged vessel (Whitewright 2011 (a), 92).

resistance which would have been provided by a deep keel (Whitewright 2011a).

Therefore, my suggestion is that, although most medieval vessels during the time of the Crusaders were lateen-rigged, they often used their sails as if they were square sails, having the yard of the sail rigged horizontally across the vessel, and not lengthwise, in the fore-and-aft manner, as one would normally do with a lateen sail. Since sailing in these times was generally downwind, there was no reason to do otherwise, and no point in using the lateen sail rigged fore-and-aft. It was also more convenient to have the yard of the lateen sail rigged across the ship, especially because changing tack or jibing is much easier with a square sail[30] than a lateen sail. Tacking with a lateen sail involves bringing the sail and the yard, which can be extremely heavy, from one side of the mast to the other, whereas tacking with a square sail only involves changing the angle of the yard and sheeting[31] the sail on the opposite side. Lateen sails could not be reefed and, in case of a strengthening wind, the sail had to be taken down and a smaller sail attached to the yard.

It is interesting to quote William of Tyre, describing the Egyptian ships which harassed Frankish coastal navigation in 1151–1153. He wrote that they were well handled, well rigged and, when sailing before the wind, had the yards of their sails crossed, which means they did not have their sails rigged fore-and-aft but across the ship. In his words: 'La navie d'Egypte emmi la mer, qui avoit si bon vent que ils venoient a pleines voiles croisées.'[32]

Lateen sails rigged across rather than fore-and-aft appear in many of the illustrations below.

In Figure 2, Bohemond and Daimbert are depicted twice: once leaving the Levant (St. Simeon?), and once arriving in Apulia (Folda 2008, 131).

The picture shows a merchant ship, probably Venetian,[33] with a sail which is depicted as triangular, attached to a cross yard at the top of a single mast. One can note that, in the top drawing, where the ship sails away from the castle, the sail is apparently attached to the yard with two lengths of line, looped around the yard, corkscrew fashion, and threaded through eyelets or grommets in the sail, in opposite directions on the port and starboard sides of the yard. In the bottom drawing, where the ship reaches Apulia, the sail is attached to the yard by a single line, looped around the yard in the same direction and threaded through grommets in the sail, in one length, from starboard to port.

---

[30] Changing tack or tacking means altering the course of the ship by bringing its bow across the wind, as opposed to jibing or wearing ship, which involves changing its course by bringing the stern across the wind. 'To tack' is 'the operation of bringing a sailing vessel head to wind and across it so as to bring the wind on the opposite side of the vessel.' (Kemp 1976, 853)
[31] 'Sheet, a purchase or a single line used for trimming a sail to the wind. A square sail set on a yard has two sheets, one to each clew (bottom corner); fore-and-aft sails have only a single sheet to the clew.' (Kemp 1976, 779)
[32] Guillaume de Tyr, XVII, 85, apud Mollat, 1967, 348.
[33] Although it seems not devoid of resemblance to Viking ships.

Figure 2. *History of Outremer.* William of Tyre, Book 11. BnF, MS Français 2628, fol. 89v.

This distinction might, obviously, be disregarded, arguing that the painter was not an expert on sails, and had not intended to be realistic. However, other illuminations in the same manuscript, by artists working in the Franco-Byzantine Crusader style (Folda 2008, 131 and 143) show the sail as an extension of the yard, without going into detail regarding manner of the sail's attachment to it (Figure 3). Indeed, most of the illustrations (apart from Figure 4, *The Voyage to Alexandria*) show lateen sails being used as square sails. Figure 4 shows the sail typically used as a fore-and-aft lateen-rigged ship (although the mast rake[34] seems to be rather exaggerated (Martin 2001, 51). The raked mast is typical of the lateen sail configuration, where the mast is often inclined, but is often un-stayed;[35] lacking ropes supporting the mast fore-and-aft), relying only on shrouds[36]. The vessel in Figure 4 boat lacks shrouds and stays.

It may be useful to stress once again that 'Recognising features of vessels in manuscript illuminations, both shipbuilding traditions and vessel components, is an inexact science.' (Flatman 2007, 23). However, this could be assisted by 'Extrapolating features from modern vessels, e.g. use of ropes and lines in standing and running rigging…' or 'extrapolating features from ethnographic examples of vessels…' (Flatman 2007, 24). Therefore, when illustrations show a triangular sail, rigged across the ship, square sail fashion, in many different images, one can assume that this is not haphazard, and that the picture does indeed reflect the manner in which the sail was used.

---

[34] 'Rake: The angle in relation to the perpendicular of a ship's mast.' (Kemp, 2005, 454)
[35] Lacking ropes or cables supporting the mast fore-and-aft.
[36] Ropes or cables supporting the mast to port (left) and starboard (right) when facing forward.

Sailing to the Holy Land

Figure 3. *Louis IX sailing east. History of Outremer*, William of Tyre, Book 34. BnF, MS Français 2628, fol. 28v.

Figure 4. Vita of St. Mark: *The Voyage to Alexandria* (c. 1275). West Vault mosaic, Zen Chapel, San Marco (Drawing after the original: C. Karmi)

Some images do show the lateen sail rigged in a proper 'lateen' fashion, as, for example, in Figure 4.

In the picture depicting Bohemond going west, which was described in *History,* the triangular sails are rigged square-sail fashion (Figure 5).

In these drawings, as in numerous other drawings, the ship is depicted with a rounded hull, with a steep sheer at bow and stern. In some of them the stern is higher and appears to support a quarterdeck and/or a castle (Figure 4 – drawing of a mosaic, and Figure 5).

Figure 5. *Retour de Bohémond 1er en Italie*. BnF, MS Français 9084

The ships in Figures 2, 4, and 5 carry sails that seem to be triangular (but possibly are not); and in Figure 5 the structure of the sail, composed of vertical strips, is very clear. The ship in Figure 4 seems to carry lateen sails.

Figure 6. Harbour scene – Kelenderis Mosaic (Photo: Prof. Levent Zoroglu, University of Konya, Turkey) (Courtesy Prof. L. Zoroglu and Dr. Zaraza Friedman)

However, the ship in Figure 5 features what could be seen as irregular elements: Although the forward rake of the foremast denotes a lateen rig, the mizzen[37] mast has a brailed-up sail. This could not actually be done on a lateen (Martin 2001; Pryor 1984, 360). Such brailing up of the sail is typical of square rigs, and was the standard method of reducing sail area when the wind strengthened, or when anchoring or mooring the ship. If the wind strengthened, the lateen sails were not reefed, but were replaced by smaller sails, a very cumbersome and difficult operation when done during a blow.

When anchoring or mooring, the lateen sails were neither reefed, nor brailed up, but taken off altogether.

When King James I of Aragon sailed to Majorca, the sailing master anticipated sudden gusts of wind:

> And he ordered the sailors to be prepared, some at the climb, some at the poop, and some others at the prow…. and when the wind came, the sailing master cried 'Lower sail! Lower sail!'….And the ships and galleys that went around us found themselves in great travail and in great difficulties trying to lower. (Smith and Buffery, 2003, 81)

This account reveals that King James' fleet practiced the reduction of sails appropriate to the lateen rig with a triangular sail, lowering the sail with its yard, rather than brailing it up, as is the usual method with a square sail. All the ships in the above illustrations have rather similar hulls, but Figure 5 shows better details of the strakes[38] curving upwards toward both ends, and perhaps clinker-built, with the strakes slightly overlapping each other, like tiles on a roof, somewhat reminiscent of Viking ships. Indeed, some scholars think that the Viking ship tradition persisted for several centuries (Bass 1972, 196), and that representations of ship types descending directly from Viking merchant ships or warships appear in manuscripts of the twelfth and thirteenth centuries.

The foremast (if there are two masts), or the single mast, in all five ships (Figures 1-5), has the slight forward rake typical of lateen rigs, in order to compensate for the lack of a forestay[39] On the two-masted ship in Figure 5, the sail on the mizzen (aft) mast is brailed up, which is much more typical of a square sail, although there is a famous example of a partially brailed-up sail on a lateener (Pomey 2006, 329), in the fifth-century ship mosaic from Kelenderis in Turkey, where a ship with a lateen-rigged sail is shown entering harbour.[40]

Nevertheless, the customary way of reducing sail in a lateener is to drop the yard to the deck, and replace the large sail by a smaller sail, rather than reefing or brailing up the large sail (Casson 1995, 268–269), and vice versa, if it is necessary to increase the sail area exposed to the wind.

The Bayeux tapestry (details in Figures 7a and b) relates to the historic events of 1064–1066, culminating in the Battle of Hastings, preceding the Crusades by about a century. It depicts ships with some attributes similar to those of

Figure 7a. *The Bayeux Tapestry* (detail) (Courtesy the town of Bayeux)

Figure 7b. *The Bayeux Tapestry* (detail) (Courtesy the town of Bayeux)

---

[37] Aft mast.

[38] Strake – planks used to construct the body of a ship.
[39] A rope or cable leading from the mast's head to the bow.
[40] This floor mosaic, depicting a brailed-up sail and reef points, unearthed by Prof. K. Levent Zoroğlu, can be viewed in www.atlasdergisi.com/ngg_tag/harbour.

Sailing to the Holy Land

Figure 8. Lateen sail (Drawing after B. Landström, C. Karmi)

Figure 9. Detail of Richard de Fournival, *Bestiaire d'Amour*, MS M.459, fol. 22r, Pierpont Morgan Library

the Crusader ship in Figure 5, and sails that appear to be triangular, but rigged in a square-sail manner, athwartship. Some researchers argue that the Bayeux ships, being of Norman origin, might have been influenced by the Viking square-sail tradition, and this might have affected both hull shape and sail shape. However, this could hardly apply to Crusader ships, mainly operated by Venetians or Genovese, nor to the Pisan merchant ships.

Sails on Crusader ships, which seem to be triangular (Figure 11), are often attached to horizontal yards. In some illustrations the yards appear to be noticeably shorter than the length of the ship (even taking into account the painter's angle of view), as opposed to lateen sails where the yard is rather long, and normally consists of at least two, or even three sections tied ('fished') together. This can be seen in Figures 8, 9, and 10.

In view of the above one may think that, maybe, the ships depicted in the illuminations of *History* are not real lateeners, but may have been ships using square sails, that are depicted as triangular either because it became a convention, or because when one looks at the bottom of the sail, which is pulled into the ship, and is seen in profile, it seems triangular, although in fact it is rectangular. Alternatively, considering that the illuminations show ships that are not otherwise typically lateen, but seem to have triangular sails, such sails may have been used in a way that imitated the square sail, namely, positioned mainly athwart (across) the ship, and not in the fore-and-aft fashion typical of the lateener (see Figures 12 et seq.) Mortes one year later, is interesting: 'En l'an apres que cil furent venus en Chipre, le roi se parti de France por passer en Aigue Morte.'[41]

---

[41] Recueil 1854, 436. Translation by the author: 'One year after having arrived in Cyprus the King left for France to arrive in Aigues Mortes.'

Figure 10. *Civitas Jerusalem* by Erhard Reuwich (detail)

Here, the painter clearly depicts a horizontally suspended sail, which does look like a square sail squeezed together at the bottom, perhaps in order to make room in the picture for the king and his entourage. Still, these sails may be triangular, in accordance with the usual custom of having lateen sails on Crusader ships.

Thus it may sometimes be difficult to distinguish between square and lateen sails. However, this is not the case for the ship illustrated in Figure 12: Its sail is obviously square.

Some examples below illustrate using a triangular sail with a square sail technique.

The image in Figure 9 (Richard de Fournival, Northern Italy, ca. 1290) is also consistent with the theory that triangular lateen sails were used in a square sail fashion. This is not only because of the way the sail is rigged, in this particular drawing, but also because the yard consists of two pieces 'fished together, typical of a lateener. However, in the present image the yards are rather short, so this leads to the possible

Figure 11. *Arrivée de Louis IX à Nicosie*. BnF, MS Français 5716, fol. 40

Figure 12. *De Re Militari* Vegetius (c. 1270) Fitzwilliam Museum Library, MS Marlay Add. 1 fol. 86r.

Figure 13(a) The Imperial fleet burns the ships of Thomas with Greek fire (thirteenth century?), from *The Illustrated Chronicle of Ioannes Skylitzes*, in Madrid (Figure 70) Biblioteca Nacional de España

Figure 13(b) Detail of *Homilies of Gregory of Nazianzus*, second half of eleventh century. Jerusalem, Patriarchal Library, Cod. Taphou 14, fol. 33r (Courtesy Jerusalem Patriarchal Library)

conclusion that showing two-piece yards was in imitation of the lateen sail fashion

What seems to be clear is that, even if the sails were triangular and designed as lateen sails, they were often not used as such, but rather as square sails. Some of the reasons for this practice have been discussed above. All the Crusader ships had great difficulties in sailing to windward[42] (Palmer 2009, mainly 323–325). The lateen sail, being a fore-and-aft sail, is supposed to enhance the upwind capability of the ship, but the hull shape of the round ship – *naves* or *salandria* – was poor, as far as lateral resistance to drift or leeway is concerned. Such ships could not really make use of the advantage supposedly offered by the lateen sail. Trying to use following winds, the Crusaders often used the triangular lateen sail as if square-rigged. This is what Ibn Jubayr called '*al-salibiyah*' (cross-like) (from Pryor 1984, Part III, 379). This could also explain why so many illustrations, illuminations or other visuals depict Crusader ships as having triangular sails attached to horizontal or oblique yards.

In Figure 14 one can see a ship apparently going upwind, since the pennant is blowing directly backward (although this a convention often adopted by inexpert illustrators). The waves also seem to be moving against the direction of sailing, judging by the bow wave breaking against the ship's stem. The ship is lateen-rigged: The sails are triangular and the masts slant typically forward. However, the sails are not sheeted in tightly, as one could expect from a ship clawing its way upwind, but fully billowed in order to take advantage of a following wind. The yards are not installed diagonally

---

[42] With the direction of the ship's movement against the direction of the wind, or, facing the wind. 'Windward' is otherwise defined as 'the weather side, or that from which the wind blows. It is the opposite side to leeward.' (Kemp 1976, 942)

Sailing to the Holy Land

with the fore low corner of the sail (the forefoot) nearly at deck level, which would help the ship advance upwind. This confusing state might explain why two sailors are shown applying their full body weight on the lines meant to bring down the yard of the main mast. One of the sailors is even shown hanging from the line after having jumped down from the aft castle.

Martin defines a lateen rig as: 'The arrangement in which a three-cornered sail is attached to a yard that obliquely crosses a low forward-raking mast.' (Martin 2001, 219) However, some of the ships are of 'mixed breed' with a triangular (or perhaps rectangular) sail attached to a cross yard, on vertical masts, in square-sail fashion. This can be seen in Figure 15.

Triangular sails apparently rigged in square-sail fashion are seen even more clearly in a miniature of the French King Philip Auguste, awaiting his fleet (Figure 16).

In the painting *St. Ursula teaching the virgins to sail* (Figure 17a), due to the following wind (indicated by the position of the flag) the skipper does not use the yard in the lateener fashion, i.e., with the front part of the yard attached to a point near the bow of the ship, but rather as a square sail, with the yard being nearly horizontal. The same seems to be the case in Figure 17b.

Figure 18 shows a galley sailing with a following wind (as shown by the direction of the flags and ensign). It has the

Figure 14. Bohemund and Daimbert, Patriarch of Jerusalem, sailing for Apulia, in a ship flying the cross of St. George (c. 1232–1261), British Library, YT 12, fol. 58v

Figure 15. The King of France and his crusading army approaching a fortress manned by Saracens, British Library Royal 19 D. I fol. 187v

Figure 16. King Philippe Auguste awaiting his fleet. *Chroniques de France ou de St Denis*, British Library Royal, MS 16 G VI, fol. 373

Figure 17a. *St. Ursula teaches the Virgins to sail*, drawing C. Karmi, after Paolo da Venezia (Muraro, fig. 84)

Figure 17b. *St. Ursula giving instructions to her companions on the voyage to Cologne.* drawing C. Karmi, after Paolo da Venezia (Muraro, fig. 87)

typical yard made of two components fished together, and could easily have proceeded with the yard set obliquely with the front end attached or close to the ship's bow. However the skipper apparently preferred to have the yard set athwartship, as if it were a square sail, the slight slant of the yard in the painting probably resulting from the need to draw it in perspective. Since the drawing dates to the early fifteenth century, the galley already has a stern rudder, along with at least one quarter rudder.

Many medieval illuminations support the theory that the Crusaders mostly used lateen-rigged ships, but used the sails as regular square sails, cross-rigged athwartship, although they were triangular sails with the apex pointing down, since their ships were not built in a manner that would allow them to benefit from a fore-and-aft rigged sail, and thus avoiding the cumbersome operation of the lateener..

Rudders and Manoeuvrability

The ship in Figure 2 is shown as having one rudder, mounted on its starboard (right) side, and there is no evidence of the existence of a second rudder on the port side. It may just be hidden because the ship is drawn in profile and we only see its starboard side. However, the existence of two quarter rudders (attached to the ship's side – near the back) may be very important for enhancing the manoeuvrability of the ship, as noted by Joinville:

> Dans ces vaisseaux de Marseille il y a deux gouvernails, qui sont attachés à deux barres si merveilleusement, qu'aussi vite que l'on aurait tourner un roussin, l'on peut tourner le vaisseau à droite & à gauche. (Joinville, 1995, 535)[43]

Figure 18. Galley of Flanders under sail (1410) (Drawing after the original, C. Karmi) [Martin 2001, 86]

On the other hand, it may also be that one of the two quarter rudders was swung up out of the water at certain points during the voyage. In order to minimize the drag and water resistance, the windward oar was raised as far out of the water as possible (Pryor 1984, Part II, 283). According to Martin, a pair of steering oars or rudders were set on the quarters of all but the smallest medieval vessels (Martin 2001, 162). Figure 2 does not specify how the rudder was attached to the hull, although this could have been done in different ways. Rather, the steering oar is merely shown protruding through the hull. This may have been the case if the rudder was mounted through the hull by a *lucatorio*, a wooden or iron ring through which the loom (handle) of the oar passes inboard (Martin 2001, 162 and 163, drawings G, H and I). However, Joinville's description seems to call for a more sophisticated means of attachment.

---

[43] "In these vessels of Marseilles there exist two rudders, which are attached to two bars [or 'rods'] in such a marvellous fashion, so that one could turn this ship right and left as fast as one could turn a horse" (author's translation).

Chapter 3

A Modern Simulation of Richard the Lionheart's Passage from Acre to Jaffa

In July 1192, about thirteen months after having first arrived in the Holy Land, King Richard I – Richard the Lionheart – decided to sail north to Beirut, en route for home (Nicholson 2005, 352). Many of King Richard's deeds in this part of the world were vividly recorded in the historical epos poem *L'Estoire de la Guerre Sainte* – the history of the Third Crusade – written in Old French by the chronicler Ambroise of Normandy. Ambroise was probably an eye-witness to many events, and accompanied the King in his travels. His rhymed couplets very poetically describe the King's actions.

Before his imminent departure, the King bade farewell to his comrades in arms of the religious military orders, the Knights Templar and the Hospitallers. Departures are often dramatic, and the situation of the King saying goodbye, while surveying the galleys, ready for tomorrow's sail, is depicted by Ambroise:

> Avait ja pris congie al Temple
> E al Hospital el contemple,
> E aveit veu ses gualees,
> Qu'eles fussent bien atornees:
> A lendemain se devait metre
> Por aler s'en, co dit la letre,
> Par Barut…
> (Ambroise 10945–10952)

This original version in Old French seems to better evoke the atmosphere of the King taking leave from the warriors who were to remain in Acre, but for easier understanding here is the English translation:

> Even Richard himself, the king
> With our own eyes we saw this thing
> Take place-had taken leave of all
> The Temple and the Hospital
> And viewed his galleys to make sure
> And on the morrow without fail
> So says the book he was to sail
> For Beirut with his retinue…[44]

As described by Ambroise, the King's galleys were ready for departure, and the fact that Ambroise uses the term 'galleys' may be important, as 'galleys' were warships and were faster than the regular cargo/passenger-carrying 'round ships'. This supports the possibility that the King was contemplating a military strike against Beirut.

However, Richard's plans for immediate departure were disrupted by the sudden arrival of messengers from Jaffa, imploring the King for urgent assistance for the Christians besieged in the citadel and facing death at the hands of the Saracens.

Ambroise very vividly describes the King sitting relaxed, awaiting his departure, when the messengers from Jaffa suddenly arrived in great haste:

> One eve the king, thus occupied,
> Sat in his tent at vespertide,
> When, lo, a vessel swiftly driven
> Came sailing into Acre haven. (10960)
> And those who disembarked stayed not,
> But straightaway the king they sought.
> Jaffa was taken, so they told
> Him, its men shut in the stronghold
> Of the Toron, where they would die
> If he his succor should deny,
> As I have told you. The good king,
> Noble in this and every thing,
> Gave up the projects he had made,
> Saying: 'I go to bear them aid,'
> (Ambroise 10963-10970)[45]

These requests for urgent help and rescue from death were received in the evening of 28 July (Gillingham 1999, 212). Richard, accompanied by Pisans and Genoese, set out immediately with a fleet which, according to Baha' al-Din (the biographer of Ṣalāḥ ad-Dīn), comprised 15 swift galleys and 35 other ships (Gillingham 1999).

After describing his hasty departure from Acre, Ambroise further depicts the troubles incurred by Richard, whose ship was trapped in Haifa Bay for three days by adverse winds.

> Such strong winds smote the band
> Upon the ships that were going to bring
> The king's companions and the king
> That for three days they had to stay
> Neath Caiphas, and there they lay
> And the king cried 'Mercy O Lord!'

> Having lost patience, Richard prayed:
> Why do you hold me and retard
> Me when I go upon your quest?

According to the Ambroise account, Richard's prayer was answered:

---

[44] In this chapter, the translations from Old French to English were made by Merton Jerome Hubert

[45] French text in Appendix I

The Lord God then did manifest
His favour sending a north wind
(Ambroise 11024–11025).[46]

Following this final good turn of events the King started on his passage to Jaffa. This offered an opportunity to test some of the descriptions of various Crusader maritime actions as an example of a passage undertaken over a short and precisely defined distance, within a specific time frame, in a known month. It encouraged me to attempt to emulate this well-documented sea journey.

Why Was Richard Held up near Haifa?

Assuming that Richard had, indeed, started out from Acre on 28 July, it may be suggested that he managed to have his galley rowed out of the Acre harbour during the evening (Gillingham 1999), when the wind is usually lighter, or blowing from the east or south-east. He may have sailed or rowed toward Haifa, but was then trapped in Haifa Bay by an adverse wind, probably south-westerly, which prevented him from continuing. According to Ambroise the King was embayed there for three days.

As already discussed above, it should be borne in mind that sailing ships cannot sail directly against the wind. A modern sailing vessel can tack upwind, sailing at an angle between 50–60 degrees off the direction of the true wind and zig-zagging right or left at the end of each leg. A very modern competitive racing yacht can sail at about 40 degrees off the true wind. However, the square-rigged ships of the eleventh and twelfth centuries could only sail with the wind from astern, or within about 45 degrees off the stern. Some could sail with the wind abeam, perhaps somewhat upwind, but not very effectively (Palmer 2009, 322–324; Whitewright 2011(a) 7-9)

Galleys were long narrow ships with a low freeboard,[47] (the distance between the waterline and the top of the ship's side), and they could not be effectively rowed against the wind for long periods (Dotson 1999, 166; 2006, 74), especially if the waves or the swell were greater than 1–1.4 m from trough to peak. Galleys also sailed well with a following wind from dead astern, but according to Dotson (2006) could not handle a quartering wind and beam sea well, where the waves hit the ship on its side. However, from the author's own sailing experience in long narrow boats, such as whalers, and even with replicas of Viking boats, a quartering wind and true beam wind would permit a galley to sail adequately, provided the sea is relatively calm and the waves not too high.

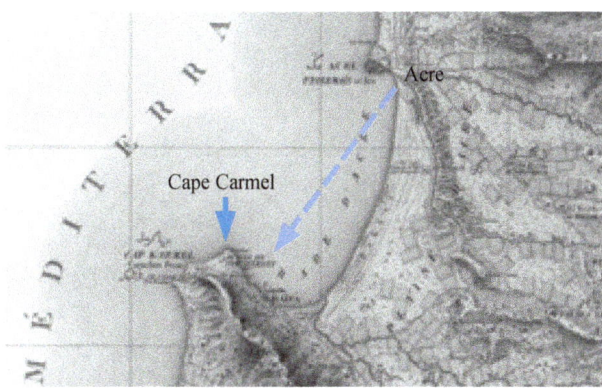

Figure 19. King Richard's probable course from Acre to Haifa (Drawing made on part of Jacotin's map)

Figure 19 shows a possible initial course taken by Richard, which he could have maintained with a north-westerly or even a westerly wind, in order to get out of Acre harbour (or anchorage), and proceed to Haifa as shown below.

However, with any of the usual prevailing winds, especially with a westerly, he could not have cleared Cape Carmel (*Ras Carmel* in Arabic). A south-south-westerly wind could have helped him clear the Cape, but would then have made sailing south toward Jaffa nearly impossible. The swell worked up by a north-westerly wind may have become substantial, so a galley would have had difficulty rowing through it, and a transport ship could not sail close-hauled, pointing into the wind. Richard therefore had to wait for the wind to change. A wind with an easterly component, favourable for a vessel embayed near Haifa, is statistically rare in both July and August. Table 1 shows the percentages of prevailing winds in July and August, according to records for Haifa in the Mediterranean Pilot.[48]

Table 1: Percentages of prevailing winds in July and August, according to records for Haifa in 1937 (Sailing Directions for the Mediterranean, 243)

	North	NE	East	SE	South	SW	West	NW	Calm
July	3	1	2	3	16	27	17	9	22
August	2	4	2	2	15	23	17	9	26

---

[46] French text in Appendix I.
[47] 'The distance measured in the waist, or centre of a ship, from the waterline to the upper deck level.' (Kemp 1976, 326) If the ship, or the boat, has no deck, then the distance measured from the waterline to the gunwale, which is 'a piece of timber going round the upper sheer strake of the boat'. (Kemp 1976, 364)

[48] There is no reason to believe that the wind patterns have changed between the twelfth century and today. This is further confirmed by Murray (1987, 139–167).
Changes in climate have been discussed by Papageorgiou (2009, 200–201), for the late Neolithic period (5300–4500 BCE); Mantzourani and Theodorou (1989), for the Bronze Age; Murray (1987), for the fourth-third centuries BCE; Pryor (1995, 208) for the Middle Ages; and Power (2002), Middle Ages, North Atlantic. It is agreed that present weather conditions can be used for interpreting earlier sailing conditions as phrased by McGrail (2001, 89): 'In the absence of more detailed knowledge of earlier Mediterranean environments, it thus seems valid to use modern data on winds, currents, tides, and coastlines to deduce the context within which Mediterranean mariners voyaged from, say, 5000 BC…until more detailed palaeo-data become generally available.'

Sailing to the Holy Land

It is clear, therefore, why King Richard had to wait and pray to the Lord. He could have been helped out of his predicament by a wind with an easterly component, preferably south-easterly or even north-easterly, which would have been rare. However, a south-south-easterly wind would get his ships out of the bay, but then would prevent him from reaching Jaffa as quickly as he did. Not only was the King obliged to await a wind that would allow him to round the Cape, but he had to be able to sail far enough west to avoid the reefs and shallows that extend into the sea from the foot of Mount Carmel. Only once out and away, could Richard's ships enjoy the northerly wind described by Ambroise, and continue south toward Jaffa.

Since it is known, in retrospect, that Richard's passage to Jaffa was apparently successful, and rather fast, a convenient wind probably helped him to weather the Cape Carmel, and, once around it, the wind probably became northerly and helped him along his way to Jaffa. So the northerly wind sent by the Lord, according to Ambroise, probably rose after Richard cleared Cape Carmel. This is consistent with the wind pattern along the coast of the Holy Land during the summer. The night is usually calm with a slight easterly off-shore breeze; which becomes southerly during the morning, veers west at noon and north-west in the afternoon. Haifa Bay can experience rather stronger easterly gusts around the Cape due to local conditions affected by the configurations of the mountain and wadi.

Some Questions about King Richard's Timetable

As mentioned above, Richard started his journey in the evening of 28 July, immediately after receiving the bad news from Jaffa. 28 July 1192 fell on a Tuesday. According to Ambroise, Richard's fleet arrived at the port of Jaffa late on Friday night, 31 July:

> They reached Jaffa late, when day
> was done, on Friday. Saturday.
> (Ambroise 11027–11028)[49]

It should have taken Richard a good few hours to get his fleet organized and sail from Acre to Haifa (6.8 nautical miles).

A wait of three days in Haifa would have been 29, 30 and 31 July. Assuming that the fleet as a whole sailed at an average speed of 4.5–5 knots (Casson 1951, 147; Whitewright 2011(a), 13), and considering the distance of nearly 50 nautical miles from Cape Carmel to Jaffa, the passage should have taken at least 10 hours under favourable conditions. Therefore it seems that, somewhere, a mistake may have been made: Either the messengers from Jaffa arrived earlier than 28 July, or Richard was not held up near Haifa for three days, or else he actually arrived off Jaffa only after midnight on Friday or early Saturday morning. Even an arrival early on Saturday would have required swift sailing with a favourable wind.

The Simulation

In order to examine probable sailing conditions of the period, I decided to try and simulate this passage in a modern yacht. A modern boat can sail upwind much better than an ancient sailing vessel, but, and on purpose, no advantage was taken of this capacity once out of Haifa Bay.

The yacht's engine was started at the fishing port of Acre on 9 August 2014, at 05.00 to get out of the harbour.[50] At the Tower of Flies the engine was stopped, and was not used again until reaching Jaffa. A 12-knot wind was blowing from the west with a slight southerly component, and in order to clear Cape Carmel I had to sail on the port tack (i.e., with the left side of the boat to the wind), as close to the wind as possible, at a speed of approximately 4.5 knots, on a course of 304°, at about 55 degrees to the true wind. With occasional puffs I progressed faster than 5 knots. In this respect I did not emulate Richard's course, as his fleet could not have sailed upwind as sharply as I did. Even a galley, which could theoretically be propelled upwind by oars, would find it difficult, if not impossible, to be rowed against the wind for any sustained period of time. Moreover, even if Richard's galley could have been propelled by oars and clear Cape Carmel, which is doubtful, one should remember that it was part of a fleet which consisted of different ships, some of which could not have been rowed around the foot of the Cape. I could have emulated King Richard's course precisely, and sailed toward Haifa, and then tacked upwind to starboard, but near the city of Haifa there are now two ports, and many ships anchored in the bay, so I preferred to tack upwind near Acre. Thus I followed the course probably taken by Richard's fleet only from a point west of Cape Carmel.

At 06.00, in a position well to the west and slightly to the north of Acre (32° 55,1'N; 035° 02,8'E) I felt that I had gained enough sea-room to clear Cape Carmel, and altered my course to 214°, with the wind still from the west, but now with a slight northerly component, blowing at 10.2 knots. From here on I sailed a course that could be held by a medieval fleet. At 07.45 (32°50,2'N; 034°57'E), with the wind still blowing from the west, with a slight northerly component, I altered course to 208°.

At 09.20 Atlit was abeam (32°43,4'N; 034°53,8'E). I had to sail further west than required in order to maintain our distance from the military base located there, obviously not a problem for King Richard. However, if his captain was a good seaman, he may have decided to sail as far as possible from the coast at this point to have a better chance of reaching Jaffa if the wind backed to the south-west. My

---

[49] Al port de Jaffe al vendresdi /Tart e par nuit le samedi

[50] I had to assume that the king's galley was rowed out of the port, and that at least part of the fleet was moored in the bay near Acre and not in the port itself. This is obvious, since, if the fleet consisted of 50 ships, and the average length of each ship was been 25–40 m, all the ships moored alongside the quay would require it to be about 1.5 km long. This is much longer than any pier or quay that existed in the ancient port of Acre. (For lengths of ships see: John H. Pryor, *The Naval Architecture of the Crusader Transport Ship*, In Mariner's Mirror, 1984, Michael of Rhodes, 2009, 214).

sailing speed was 4 knots, the wind still westerly with a slight northerly component. The fact that the wind did not back to the southwest at this time of the year and at this hour was unusual, but I had enough distance from the coast to allow me to cope with a southwesterly should it arise, so I altered course to 191°, which was about 100° off the true wind. This course was also convenient in view of the coastal configuration: Jaffa is west of Acre and the line of the coast runs northeast–southwest, at about 200°.

At 12.15 I was opposite Caesarea, sailing at 4.5 knots, wind 11.5 knots northwest, the course still 191°.

At 16.30, I approached Apollonia-Arsuf, and tried to sail closer to the shore to have a better view of the castle. (It was roughly behind the area where the castle is located that on 7 September 1191, King Richard won the famous Battle of Arsuf against the Ayyubid armies of Salah ed-Din.) The wind was blowing at 13 knots from 330° and yacht's speed exceeded 5 knots.

At 18.00, the wind died, as expected, and became northerly, 2–4 knots.

At 18.20, the wind picked up somewhat. I was opposite Jaffa harbour, at Andromeda's Rock. The entrance between the present breakwater and Andromeda's Rock is easy to see, but to enter safely today, it is advisable to line up two minarets seen from the sea, one close to the shore and one further away. Following this line will take the vessel clear of the rocks at the entrance to the port and into the harbour.

Figure 20 shows the general progress of the trip.

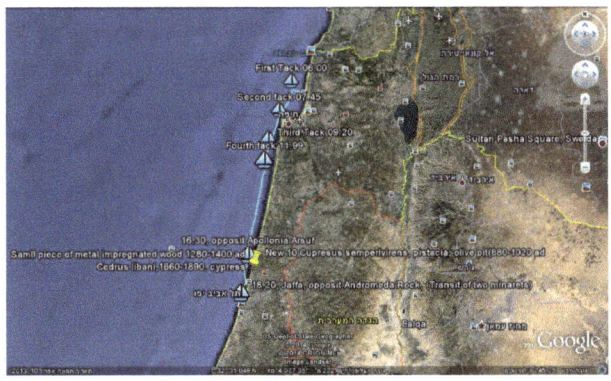

Figure 20. Progress of author's passage simulating King Richard's passage from Acre to Jaffa
(The yellow marker shows the location of an underwater find which may indicate the existence of a wreck; see below)

However, Richard probably did not land at Jaffa port, but rather on the beach north of it. The map (Figure 21) shows my course in greater detail, with the direction of the wind at various hours represented by light blue arrows.

If the story told by Ambroise is more or less correct (and the major facts are corroborated by Baha' al-Din), then this short passage proves that Richard's fleet was manned by skilful seamen, consisting of Genovese and Pisan sailors, and perhaps also seamen who came with Richard from England. It may be deduced that substantial fleets could have been launched on their way at short notice and stayed in close formation, since many ships arrived in Jaffa at the same time, as described below, and could cover substantial distances in a relatively short time.

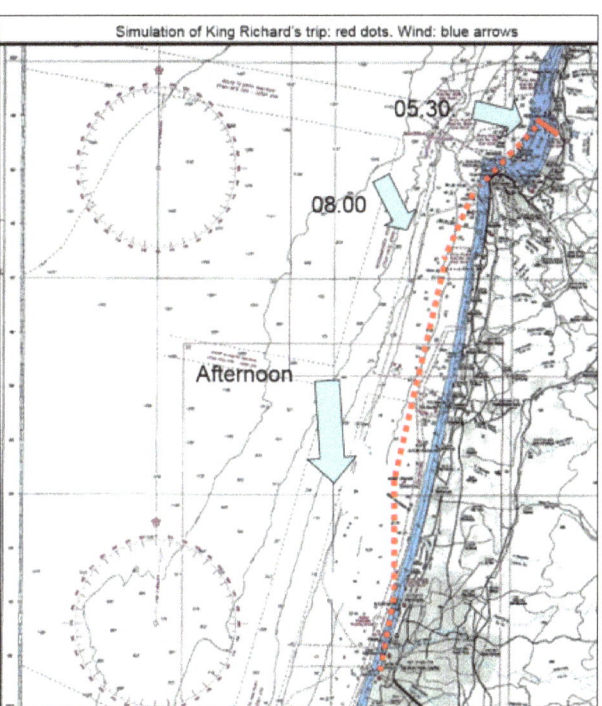

Figure 21. Progress of the author's passage simulating King Richard's passage from Acre to Jaffa with reference to winds (on marine chart) (Courtesy Survey of Israel)

The fact that King Richard's galleys reached Jaffa after about 10 hours of sailing from Cape Carmel, disproves the supposition that Crusader ships could sail properly only with a wind dead astern (Dotson, 2006). According to all the available data (for example Watts 1975, 568), as well as my experience, it is unlikely that Richard enjoyed a pure northerly wind throughout the passage. Winds always shift, and since Richard arrived late at night, it is possible, but obviously not certain, that for a few hours at least the wind may have had an easterly component. The conclusion should therefore be that the galleys, as well as the other ships in King Richard's fleet, could have advanced reasonably well during the passage from Cape Carmel to Jaffa with any kind of a following wind and, to some extent, also with a beam wind.

This simulated passage also proves that, given the same circumstances, and some luck with the winds, 800 years ago vessels could achieve the same result as a modern yacht and Ambroise's description of Richard's passage reflected the truth.

Landing in Jaffa

When the Turks saw the galleys approaching the port:
The Turks observed the port, and they

Could see that there the galleys lay.
(Ambroise 11079 –11080).

They, the 'Turks', rushed to the shore with bucklers and shields, on foot and on horseback, to forestall Richard's landing (Ambroise 11080–11083; Nicholson 1997, 355).

It should be noted that the first ships to approach the shore in order to land were indeed 'galleys', and not cogs, round ships or other transport vessels. It is true that the word 'galley' was sometimes used generically for all kinds of ships, but Ambroise knows the difference: When he chooses he writes about a 'nef'.

> E a lor **nefs** a plein alouent (Ambroise 10943)
> Would seek their **ships** without delay

Or a barge:

> Eth vos une barge abrivee
> Venir a Acre e arrive
> (Ambroise 10958-10959)
> When, lo, a **vessel** swiftly driven
> Came sailing into Acre haven.

It is obvious that the first ships that made it to Jaffa could only be galleys, which could be beached, because it is said that the king jumped off his ship into the water, after having taken off his leg-armour ('the leap which won him a place in Paradise,' Gillingham, 1999, 213). Richard then waded ashore, the water reaching up to his belt, as described by Ambroise:

> He sent the galleys closer. Stripped
> The armor from his legs and leaped
> Into the sea, which came waist-high
> By happy chance. So to the dry
> Land he pushed boldly on in front
> Second or first, as was his wont.
> (Ambroise 11127–11132).[51]

Entering Jaffa's so-called 'port' with the fleet would have been impossible, because of the port's small size, and the difficult and dangerous entrance (Mirkin 2017, 139-143). In order to enter the port, ships had to be propelled by oars only, or else towed, which, for vessels other than galleys, would be extremely difficult, if not impossible. The conclusion therefore is that when King Richard, and probably most other Crusaders, refer to landing at the 'Jaffa Port' they probably landed on the beach, north of the modern mooring basin.

In this area the beach slopes gently, and the approach from the north is free of rocks, whereas to the south of the port there was a line of rocks. This line begins with Andromeda's Rock at the entrance to the port, and continues south, under the present-day breakwater built over the rocks during the British Mandate, and then again further south beyond the breakwater.

The fact that the water reached up to Richard's belt proves that the ship (a shallow-draught galley) that landed him was quite close to the beach, where the water was about 1 m deep: some sources note that the water reached up to his groin (Nicholson 1997, 355).

> After wading ashore the King was followed by
> Geoffrey du Bois, Peter de Preaux, and the rest of his force:
> (Ambroise 11131 – 11135).
> Land he pushed boldly on in front,
> Second or first, as was his wont.
> Geoffrey du Bois also landed:
> The King's good man, Pierre de Preaux
> And all the rest were not far back;
> They came together to attack.
> (Ambroise 11131 – 11136).

Another description of Richard's landing appears in the *Itinerarum*: 'Galeis igitur regis ad imperium versus littus propulsis' (*Itinerarum, Liber VI, Capitulum XV*, 408). In translation: 'The word was forthwith given, the galleys were pushed to land' (*Itinerary*, Book 6, ch XV, 264). In a different translation:'…the galleys were driven towards the shore' (Nicholson 1997, 355). The latter seems to agree more with the Latin text.

Such a forceful landing, which, as Ambroise relates, managed to chase away the Turks who had occupied the shore, could only have been made by beaching the galleys on the shore, and probably awaiting further forces on other ships to be landed by skiffs and other small craft.

May I deduce that this was the usual method the Crusaders used to create a beachhead on a hostile shore?

---

[51] French text in Appendix I

Chapter 4

Crusader Fleet Seamanship

Keeping Order

There is very little contemporary information about seamanship of Crusader fleets and their conduct and management at sea.

We can only study the subject by examining materials from a later date, for example, the fourteenth-century *Book of Michael of Rhodes,* or from descriptions of Crusader activities other than those relating to the Holy Land, mainly their actions against the Saracens in Spain, the Balearic Islands, or Constantinople.

The chronicler in the *Book of Deeds of James I of Aragon* (1208-1276) devotes special attention to the 'manner the fleet should proceed' (Smith and Buffery 2003, 79):

> At the front Bovet's ship...was to serve as a guide, and had to carry a lantern as light; whilst Carros's ship had the rearguard and carried another lantern...And the galleys had to go around the outside of the fleet, in such manner that if another galley came it would encounter our galleys. (Smith and Buffery 2003, 79).

> The fleet itself was composed of 'twenty-five full ships, eighteen *tarides* and twelve galleys, and one hundred *buzas* and *galliots*. And so there were one hundred and fifty big vessels, without counting the small barques. (Smith and Buffery 2003, 78)

Keeping order in the fleet was, and is, of prime importance. This was certainly difficult in a fleet composed of various types of ships as, for example, King Richard's fleet sailing from Messina to the East, when:

> The king had laid down that as far as possible the ships should never be separated, unless they were scattered in a storm. So the galleys deliberately reduced their speed in an attempt to stay with the flotilla of slower transport vessels. (Nicholson 1997, 174)

> The task of keeping together obviously became more difficult at night, so ships had to carry lanterns. It was King Richard's custom to '...have in his ship an enormous lighted candle in a lantern, which was placed aloft to give light to all around and show the sailors the way'.[52] (Nicholson 1997, 175)

Lantern signals were probably also the basic means of conveying orders by night. This was valid in the fifteenth century, when Michael of Rhodes[53] wrote, in his instructions:

> sailing by night
> And he commands that if he wishes to set the large sail he will make two fires on the fireplace, one on each side. And if he wishes to set the middle sized sail he will likewise make three fires on the hearth and all galleys must respond to these signals under penalty of [one] hundred soldi, and let no one dare pass the captain, under whatever penalty shall please him. (Long et al. 2009, vol. II, 329)

As noted, little is told directly about how such fleets were organised, and how the mixture of types of vessels carrying mounted knights and their horses were able to coordinate with galleys that were propelled by sails or oars. Did fleets manage to stay in formation, in spite of the fact that the round ships could probably withstand rough seas much better than galleys, and large ships had to keep the same pace as small ships?

However, tight cooperation was essential and was implemented, as, for example, in the campaign of James I of Aragon for the conquest of Majorca: Oar-propelled galleys towed *tarides* which (as opposed to the *tarides* of Charles I of Anjou) were propelled by sails only:

> And when it was midnight you would have said that in our entire fleet not a sound was heard. And each of the twelve galleys left, towing its taride, and they continued towing the tarides from the port little by little. (Smith and Buffery 2003, 83).

The story of the war against the Saracens in Almeria, Spain, during the Second Crusade can serve as an example of the way a fleet was handled; for example the account of the Genoese expedition to Spain during the Second Crusade, which was written very soon after the events in question. The author, Caffaro di Rustico (1080–c. 1164), was one of the leading men of Genoa. He served as a consul of the city six times between 1122 and 1149, and as consul, commanded a naval expedition to Minorca in 1146.

In 1147 the Genoese were ordered to prepare for war against Almeria, which was the principal port for Cordoba, the traditional capital of Islamic Spain. Almeria is located about 170 km east of Malaga, and its possession would give the Genoese a base for penetrating the markets of Al-Andalus. The Genoese started their journey with 63 galleys and 163

---

[52] It seems that King Richard, who wanted to have 'light all around', was not unduly worried about night blindness. In later years as, for instance, during the Napoleonic wars, the British Navy always used shaded lanterns for such purposes.

[53] The Book of Michael of Rhodes, A Fifteenth Century Maritime Manuscript, edited by Pamela O. Long, David McGee and Alan M. Stahl, Vol. II. A Venetian mariner's illustrated manuscript, it includes a treatise on mathematics, treatments of contemporary shipbuilding practices, navigation, calendrical systems, and astrological ideas.

'other vessels'. Caffaro does not specify which other vessels were part of this huge fleet, but:

> ...after they had come at Porto Maone, the consul Balduino went ahead to Almeria with fifteen galleys as an advance guard until the fleet should arrive as a body. The Genoese arrived at Capo de Gato but not finding the 'emperor'[54] they waited there for a month in a state of great fear, since they were outside the port. (Caffaro di Rustico 2009, 3)

Fleet action apparently could involve combined sea and land operations, as can be learned from the following:

> The consul Balduino, who was on guard with his galleys, then ordered his companions, namely Oberto Torre and Philippo and Ansaldo Doria, to come and make war against Almeria. These companions were unhappy about [doing] this, until some troops should arrive. Meanwhile the Count of Barcelona came with a great ship, bringing soldiers with him, including fifty-three mounted knights. They sent a message to Balduino that he should arrive at the mosque with his galleys at daybreak and make a demonstration of wishing to do battle, so that the Saracens should leave the city for this, for the count and his knights would be at the river at dawn, on land. The fifteen galleys would be outside the [River] Lena and one galley would be stationed at the mouth of the Lena. After the Saracens came out to fight, that galley would give the signal to the knights and the fifteen [other] galleys. And so it was done.[55] (Caffaro di Rustico 2009, 4)

Caffaro continues his description of the combined operations: sea, land and mounted knights arriving by sea in the following passage:

> Once the Saracens saw the men from the fifteen galleys going ashore, apparently intent on doing battle, they were afraid that there were others hiding in secret. Thus they sent two soldiers, one white and one black, to climb up onto a hillock and reconnoitre the surrounding area. They did not spot the soldiers who were in hiding, and so they made a signal with flags for the Saracens to sortie from the city and come to do battle. Forty thousand armed men promptly emerged and began to fight with the men from the fifteen galleys. The Genoese then boarded the galleys and remained there, with eight of their men being killed. Meanwhile the consul Ansaldo Doria, on the one galley that was on watch, made the signal, even though it was not at the proper time. Twenty-five galleys and the knights all set off as one, and these galleys came across others, took them along with them and acted in unison. The consuls Oberto Torre and Philippo, who were off Capo de Gata, set sail with the whole fleet. They sailed forwards with twelve galleys as a vanguard, while on land the knights [marched off]. These twelve galleys made contact with the others which were at the mosque, and they moved forwards to the coast. The knights then encountered the Saracens who had left the city, and fortified by Divine assistance, they manfully attacked them. For fear of the galleys the Saracens wished to turn back, and they started to retreat towards the city, with the knights following them. ... The aforesaid consuls promptly went ashore with the men from one galley to fight the Saracens, and the men who manned the galleys near the mosque also landed. They and the knights killed more than five thousand Saracens and left them lying dead along the shore. The galleys that were out to sea also joined the battle and they killed the Saracens fleeing to seaward...

> After some discussion, the consuls decided that the galleys should be beached on the shore at Almeria, and after this had been done they gave instructions for the preparation of siege engines, towers and 'cats'... (Loud, in Jansen et al. 2009, 119–120)

All of the above obviously show a high degree of coordination, transmission of orders and discipline. It can also be deduced from the text that coordination existed between naval forces and the mounted knights, and that beaching the galleys was a common practice. In addition, it can be understood that there were means to disembark knights and horses without a harbour, at the mouth of the River [Lena].

The above, however, does not specify at all how horses were landed and troops disembarked:; it simply seems to take for granted that such operations were carried out without specifying the manner. We will deal with this question below.

Skiffs and Other Small Boats

Whatever fleet management method was adopted, nothing could be accomplished without the use of many small boats. It is obvious that whatever the vessel – oared galley, round ship or dromon – it was often accompanied by small boats, whether on board, towed behind or alongside, or both.

Some galleys could land on shore, being relatively light and shallow-draught. They could also approach a pier or a jetty, whether alongside or, perhaps even in what is called today: 'Mediterranean style' – stem or stern on to the jetty, and the other end held by one or more anchors to seaward. However, large ships could hardly land on the beach, and if they did, it is not at all clear how they could

---

[54] King Alfonso VII of Castile (1126–57), who claimed to be Emperor of all Spain, had concluded an alliance with Genoa in September 1146, to the effect that they would jointly besiege Almeria in the following May, and contributing 10,000 *marobotini* towards the costs of outfitting the Genoese fleet, *Codice diplomatico della repubblica di Genova dal (dcclviii al mclxiii*, ed. C. Imperiale di Sant'Angelo (*Fonti per la storia d'Italia*, Rome 1936), 204–9 nos. 146–7. In fact the attack took place in August 1147, and Almeria was captured on October 17. Cf. Caffaro di Rustico 2009, 3.

[55] This text was translated from *Annali Genovesi di Caffaro e de'suoi continuatori*, ed. L.T. Belgrano (*Fonti per la storia d'Italia*, Rome 1890, 79–89), by G.A. Loud. There also exists a translation, by Martin Hall and Jonathan Philips, in *Caffaro, Genoa and the Twelfth-Century Crusades I*. Dorchester 2013, 127–136. However, the translation by Loud somehow seems more contemporary, and seems to reflect the flavour of the original text better.

be towed back out to sea. (This is discussed further in the section dealing with landing or beaching.) Many ports were small and not accessible to ships, or even to galleys, except for very small skiffs, as, for instance, the 'port' of Apollonia-Arsur (or Arsuf). Lacking the manoeuverability of an oared galley, a pure sailing vessel must have loaded and unloaded horses, and even people or merchandise by lighter, a difficult operation to carry out in a hostile harbour or beach (Martin 2002, 242).

Ample reference to the use of skiffs or other small boats is found in many texts referring to maritime action by Crusaders: When Richard the Lionheart fought Isaac Duke Comnenus, pretender to the title of Emperor of Cyprus, Richard was offended by Comnenus, who had scorned his emissaries, and immediately shouted an order to all his forces: 'to arms': 'They immediately obeyed. When he was armed he and all his people rowed forward in small boats called *snekas* to seize the port.' (Nicholson 1997, 183–184). However, the battle was not quickly resolved, and after an initial success Richard's men came under severe attack by crossbowmen.

> The king, realizing that our people were not bold enough to get out of the skiffs and advance on the shore, took the lead himself in jumping out of his barge into the sea, and boldly attacked the Griffons. (Nicholson 1997, 185)

Modern sailing yachts need an auxiliary engine to enter a marina, or go alongside a pier, although they are much more manoeuvrable than the medieval ship. A vessel could enter a bay, the Bay of Acre, for example, spill the wind from its sail, or turn into the wind, and drop an anchor or anchors. However, without assistance it could not safely negotiate the entrance to a port or approach a quay without damaging itself or other vessels or installations.

Small Boats in the Seventh Crusade

'Small boats' were not always small, and by comparison with boats that served other known ships, it can be deduced that some of the boats ordered as ships' boats from Genoa by Louis IX, could have been more than 10 m long, and carried 52 oars (Pryor, 1984, 372). Since such ships' boats could not be carried on board, the contract for building the *Paradisus,* the flagship of Louis IX, specified that the cable to tow the ship's boat should be a new one (Pryor, 1984, 373), obviously because a new cable would be more resistant to the wear and tear involved in towing. Other boats, such as gondolas, or the *barca de parischalmo*, were indeed smaller, and therefore must have been carried on board (Pryor 1984).

Among the many tasks allocated to boats towed behind the ship was also that of a prison cell. According to Joinville, Louis IX instructed that some sons of a certain 'Bourgeois', be imprisoned on the *barje de cantier* a boat towed behind the ship, because they delayed the fleet's departure from Panteleria by eating 'fruits des jardins'. The youths started to weep, pleading not to be placed in the boat where 'les murtriers et les larrons were imprisoned.'[56] (Joinville 1867, 432). The custom of towing a ship's boat was not typical only of Crusaders: When Ibn Jubayr sailed from Acre in 1184 one of the ship's spars broke and fell into the sea. The longboat attached to the ship was manned by sailors, and used to retrieve it (Broadhurst 1951, 328).

In conclusion, it is clear that small craft, whether carried on board or towed behind the mother ship, served several purposes: They were absolutely necessary for watering the ships – bringing water from a well, spring or other source to a ship anchored offshore, they acted as landing craft, they were used for communication between the ships in the fleet, they may have acted as lifeboats, and the *barje de cantier* even had a cauldron installed.

Jacques de Vitry (c. 1160–1240), who was appointed bishop of Acre, encountered some very rough seas during his trip to the Holy Land. In a letter describing his adventurous trip and the storm which threatened to sink the ship in which he sailed he wrote:

> quidam autem nautarum michi compatientes et deferentes ut navem parvam, que magne navi alligata erat.[57]

This demonstrates the custom of towing a boat behind the ship, as can be seen in the fifteenth-century miniature, Figure 22.

The use of small boats to unload equipment and chests to a military campsite, along a shore or a beach without a quay, wharf, pier or installation is depicted in *The Landing of Hannibal in Africa*, Figure 23.

On the other hand, *The Siege of Orikos by Philip of Macedonia and the Romans*, and *The Landing of the Greeks in Troy*, show the use of small boats for debarkation of troops on a hostile beach (Figures 24 and 25).

Small boats were also used to send messengers, as for instance when King Baldwin approached Jaffa. The top half allegedly depicts Baldwin's battle in Ramla). The small boat, apparently sent by the mother ship flies a white flag (Probably the flag of the Kingdom of Jerusalem, which was white with a yellow cross and four crosslets (Figure 26).

> Use of small boats as lifeboats is mentioned in many chronicles, such as Felix Fabri's *Book of Wanderings of Brother Felix Fabri,* when his ship was wrecked near the coast of Dalmatia: '…and there was a great crush on the companion ladders and a hurried rush of everybody

---
[56] Murderers and thieves.
[57] Some of the sailors, feeling sorry for me and showing their respect, tried to persuade me to enter a little boat that had been attached to the great ship, but I absolutely refused to comply because of the bad example [that this would set], for I wanted to experience the common danger with the others *(Vitry* 1960, 44*)*.

Figure 22. *Departure of Ulysses*, Riccardiano 492, Publio Virgilio Marone, Bucolica, Georgica Anneis, Sec.XV, sesto decennio, Biblioteca Riccardiana, Firenze

Figure 23. *Débarquement de Hannibal en Afrique* (1493?). BnF, MS Français 366, fol. 114

Figure 24. *Siege of Orikos by Philippe of Macedonia* (1493?). BnF, MS Français 366, fol. 54v

towards the stern to get into the boats which had been launched'. (Fabri 1896, 43)

In addition to all these tasks, small boats could tow ships not equipped with sweeps or oars. They could even be used to tow the ship around a headland, if there was no wind, or, sometimes, even against the wind, if the conditions allow and the rowing crew was very strong.[58] The small boats could assist the mother ship in sailing out of a congested harbour, moving away from a pier and, in some cases, helping to prevent it being dragged onto a lee shore. They could also

---

[58] Eighteenth-century ships were known to be towed by their boats for days when becalmed in the Doldrums.

Figure 25. *Le débarquement des Grecs à Troie* (1400?). BnF, Français 301, fol. 58v

Figure 27. Small boat helping to retrieve an anchor. Bodleian Library Auctarium MS D 4.17, fol. 1v

Figure 28. *Louis of France arriving in England*, from Matthew Paris OSB, *Chronica maiora II.* (Mid-thirteenth century), Parker Library, Corpus Christi College in Cambridge, MS 161 fol. 46v (new folio number f 50 v)

Figures 27–33 are medieval illuminations and miniatures dated between the twelfth and fifteenth centuries, showing combinations of sailing vessels and small boats which either assist people in landing, or are towed behind sailing ships, or help to load or unload ships or accompany larger vessels.

Figure 28 shows how a small boat helped King Louis disembark from his ship.

The three miniatures, Figures 31–33, demonstrate the fact that ships were often accompanied by small boats, which are seen here near the ships, so one can assume that they were being towed or about to be towed.

Naval Support of Land Operations

All the countries in the Levant, including Palestine, have long coastlines. Hence, while roads were not always good, sometimes traversing dangerous narrow passages, like that between Cape Carmel and the coast, swamps and other obstacles, the sea offered space where troops and siege engines, as well as mounted knights, could be transported without much hindrance. Similarly to air supremacy today, one could say that the ruler of the sea also ruled the coast. The ruler of the coast also controlled the important access points to the interior of the country, such as Jaffa and Acre, to some extent.

Figure 26. *King Baldwin's battle in Ramla* (top), and *Approaching Jaffa* (bottom) (1474) BnF, MS Français 5594, fol. 109

assist in manoeuvring, laying or retrieving anchors, and so forth as, for instance, in Figure 27.

A substantial number of small oared craft was essential to the functioning of any kind of fleet. According to the chronicler John de Columna, the mariners of Louis IX who waited in Cyprus for the Crusade to be launched, spent the winter of 1248–1249 in repairing and building small boats for landing operations (Wolff and Hazard 1969, 494).

Sailing to the Holy Land

Figure 29. *Loading of St. Mark's relics in Alexandria.* Mosaic, Saint Clemente Chapel, San Marco (first half of twelfth century. Drawing after original C. Karmi)

Figure 30. *Loading ships for the Crusade* (1352). BnF, MS Français 4724, fol. 6

Figure 31. Edward III sets sail to relieve Thouars. *Chroniques Jean Froissart* (1410). The Hague, KB, 72 A 25 fol. 349v

Advancing and holding the coast could not be accomplished without close cooperation between land and sea forces. Thus, the Crusaders failed when such cooperation was lacking, as for example, at Arsuf in 1099, Caesarea in 1102 and Ascalon in 1106. They succeeded at Arsuf in 1101, with the support of the Genoese fleet, and in Caesarea in 1102, when King Baldwin of Jerusalem came with all his forces by land, and the ships proceeded along the coast.[59] They also succeeded in Haifa (Caiffa) in August 1100, when the Venetian fleet overcame the resistance of the town's defenders (Grousset 1934, Vol. I, 258). The Hospitaller fleet probably assisted and transported men and provisions of its order to the vicinity of Acre, which was then besieged by the Christian forces of the Third Crusade (Jacoby 2007b, 58).

On his march to Arsur, Richard the Lionheart advanced southward along the coast from Caesarea, and received supplies ferried by sea (Erlich 2014, 115); his forces being repeatedly resupplied by the fleet, which kept pace with the army (Kedar 2015, 118).

The role played by naval forces was also reflected in works composed after the fact, for example, *La Chanson d'Antioche*, now known in a version composed about 1180 for a courtly French audience, and embedded in a quasi-historical cycle of epic poems, inspired by the events of 1097–1099, the climax of the First Crusade. It describes the conquest of Antioch and Jerusalem and the origins of the Crusader states. The *Chanson* was reworked in the fourteenth century and incorporated into an extended Crusade cycle, which embroidered the events to a great extent.

The *Chanson d'Antioche* illustrates the importance of the Crusaders' naval support as seen through the eyes of the Saracens, albeit with a slight exaggeration: Garsion, King of Antioch, sends his son, Sansadoine, to the King of Soudan to ask for help, since, apparently 'no French Christians remained anywhere that are not in the ships assisting in the siege of his city':

> Tu lui diras qu'il vienne me secourir avec son armée
> Car il n'est pas resté des Français dans la chrétienté
> Qui n'est passe outre-mer sur des navires
> Ils ont assiégé Antioche, la belle cité
> Ils seront assez puissants pour aller jusqu'à la Mecque.
> (*Chanson d'Antioche*, Chant XVIII, 220)[60]

In order for the king of Soudan to believe that the message is genuine, so says the story, Garsion shaved one side of his own beard and gave it to his son, as a proof of its veracity.

Naval support was essential to many, if not all, land operations; thus they were recounted not only in legendary epics, but also by chroniclers:

---

[59] 'Le roi vint avec tout son ost par terre, et la navie l'aloit costoiant par la mer,' *Guillaume de Tyr et ses continuateurs.* (Mollat 1967, 347)

[60] You will tell him to come and save me with his army
Because no Frenchman remained in Christendom
Who did not cross the Outremer aboard ships
They laid siege to Antioch, the beautiful city,
They will be powerful enough to go on to Mecca
(translation by the author).

The leaders of the First Crusade chose the land route, but even they needed marine or naval help, not only for crossing rivers and the Bosphorus, but also, on a smaller scale, for military operations. When they attempted to take Nicée (Nicaea, probably Iznik of today) located about 100 km south-east of Constantinople, at the time the capital of the Sultanate of Rüm, their attempts were foiled by the fact that the Turks brought supplies across the lake that borders the city from the west. The Crusader leaders asked the emperor to send boats to the port of Civitot, located in the south-eastern corner of the Sea of Marmara, and from there the boats were dragged by oxen, approximately 15 km to Lake Iznik, where the Crusaders used them to stop the Turkish shipping, which allowed them to take the town. This story is told by the anonymous author of the History of the First Crusade:

> Tunc nostri majores, consiliati in unum, miserunt nuntios Constantinopolim, dicturos imperatori ut faceret naves conduci ad Civitot, ubi portus est, atque juberet congregari boves qui eas traherent per montanas et silvas approximent lacui. (*Histoire Anonyme*, 40)[61]

The author of the *Itinerary of Richard* recounts the importance of naval assistance in a chapter entitled 'How our ships brought us provisions from Acre to Joppa'.

> The army remained outside the walls of Joppa, and refreshed themselves with abundance of fruits, figs, grapes, pomegranates, and citrons, produced by the country around: when lo! the fleet of King Richard, with other vessels, which accompanied the army and went to and fro between Joppa and Acre, brought us necessaries, much to the annoyance of the Turks, because they could not prevent them. (*Itinerary*, Book IV, Chapter XXV, 189)[62]

Combined sea and land operations are well described by Guillaume de Villehardouin, when he writes about the conquest of Constantinople. It was agreed that the French would attack by land, and the Venetians by sea, because the city is like a ship's sail (*voile de nav*): one part is on land and the other on the sea (Buchon 1845, 13). The details are interesting because, as Villehardouin explains, the sea is deep there so the ships can come right up to the walls of the city: 'Donc, Donc pour ce que la mer est si profonde que les navs viegnent rez a rez de terre, si s'ariverent li Venicien…et venoient droit sus les murs de la ville.' (Buchon 1845, 88)[63]

Villehardouin renders a vivid description of the importance of naval forces when planning the conquest of Monemvasia

---

[61] 'Then our superiors, having come to a unanimous decision, sent messengers to Constantinople, who will tell the emperor to have the ships assembled at Civitot, where there is a harbour, and tell him to order that oxen be collected, who would pull the ships through the forested mountains to the edge of the lake.' (Translation by the author)
[62] The full title of this work is: *Richard of the Holy Trinity, Itinerary of Richard I and others to the Holy Land* (formerly ascribed to Geoffrey de Vinsauf).
[63] 'so, since the sea is so deep that if the ships come to the level of the land, if the Venetians arrive they will come right up to the walls of the city.' (Translation by the author)

Figures 32–34. Three miniatures (early fifteenth century) British Library, Harley 4431, *The Book of the Queen*, fol. 196v

Sailing to the Holy Land

(Malevesie) and Naples (probably today's Nau[v]plion), both in the Peloponnese. Both are important harbours that had to be conquered due to the trouble they caused the Crusaders as bases for the Greek navy:

> Mais encore avons à conquester deux forteresses, les quelles nous griévant moult en cest pays; c'est le chastel de Naples qui cy pres de nous est, et Malevesie; car ce sont li maistre port et l'escale des vaisseaux des Grex. (Buchon 1845, 88)[64]

Guillaume goes on to say that if these strong places are not taken and are besieged only by land, it would be a forlorn hope because they (the besieged) will have all they want from the sea:

> …li chastel estoient si fort, qui les assiegeroit par terre, que ce seroit paine perdue, pour ce qu'il auroint par mer toutes leyrs volantés. Mais qui à droit les voudroit assiegier, il convendroit mettre le siege par terre et par mer; et ainsi porroit on venir à son entendement. (Buchon 1845, 89)[65]

June 1191 found King Richard the Lionheart after his victorious sojourn in Cyprus. Knowing that Acre was besieged, and perhaps about to fall to the Crusaders (Nicholson 1997, 196), he made haste to sail there so that the conquest of Acre would not take place without him. On his way he encountered a very large Saracen ship, which tried to hide its identity by a *ruse de guerre*, pretending that it was a Genoese vessel heading for Tyre. When the ruse did not work a battle developed between Richard's galleys and the Saracen ship, but the latter was so large that the galleys could not overcome it. The only solution was for some of Richard's sailors to dive under the ship and tie its rudder with ropes, which slowed the ship down, and probably caused it to sail around in circles:

> Cil saillirent come tempest,
> Si se plungierent cors e teste,
> Par de soz la nef trespasserent
> E repaiererent e ralerent:
> As governels liierent cordes,
> Por els destorbere plaisier
> E por la nef plus abaissier[66]
> (Ambroise 2229–2235)

Figure 35. Crusaders attack Acre, Florence, Bibl. Medicea-Laurenziana, fol. 292r, Book 24, ch. 1

After overcoming fierce resistance in the ensuing battle, the Saracen ship was rammed and sunk, and Richard explains that if this had not happened – and the Saracen ship (which carried elite troops, and among other things, two hundred deadly serpents), Acre could not have been taken: Se fust en Acre la nef mise/Jameis ne fust la citié prise[67] (Ambroise 2277–2278).

The conquest of Acre with the help of naval forces is shown in Figure 35.

A Spectacular Naval Attack in the Fifth Crusade

Many attempts were made to conquer the city of Damietta, located in the Nile Delta. Amalric took Damietta during the Second Crusade in 1164, and again during the Third Crusade (1196–1197). A very well-documented attempt to conquer Damietta took place during the Fifth Crusade. Initiated by Pope Innocent III, this Crusade was intended to travel by sea. The pope recognized the prime importance of avoiding the problems of the Fourth Crusade, and thus caused a truce to be made between Venice and its old adversary Padua, which freed the Venetians to transport large numbers of Crusaders from two different starting points: Messina and the Apulian coast of Italy, thus not overloading a single port.

Innocent also issued a declaration that 'Corsaires, pirates and others guilty of molesting and despoiling pilgrims en route to the Holy Land were to be excommunicated' (Sterling 2003, 110). Innocent died on 16 July 1216, one year before the Crusade was scheduled to depart, while working on a political dispute between Genoa and Pisa. His successor,

---

[64] 'But we still have to conquer two fortresses that cause us much grief (trouble) in this country; It is the castle of Naples which is near us, and Malevesie; because these are the principal harbours and stop-overs of the Greek vessels.' (Translation by the author)

[65] 'The castles are so strong, that to lay siege to them by land will be forlorn hope, because they will be able to receive all that they desire by sea. But he who would like to besiege them properly, the siege should be laid by land and by sea; and thus one could reach the desired goal.' (Translation by the author)

[66] 'Then like a tempest on they drove/ And headfirst in the water dove/ Beneath the ship; on the other side/ They swam back, and deftly tied/ The ropes that to the helm were bound/ Of the pagan ship, so to confound/ The infidels, to make them steer/ Awry, and cause their craft to veer.' (Translation: Merton Jerome Hubert)

[67] 'Had the ship come to Acre, 'tis plain/ The town would never have been ta'en.' (Translation: Merton Jerome Hubert)

Figure 36. Siege of Damietta, 1248, Mathew Paris. *Chronica Maiora*, Parker Library, Corpus Christi College, Cambridge, fol. 59V, MS 16II

Honorius III, although dedicated to the Crusader effort, was unable to foster real peace and unity among all the contingents (Sterling 2003, 110). Nevertheless, a crusading army commanded by John de Brienne, consisting of warriors of many European countries, was assembled in Acre, and a decision was reached to attack Damietta first. The idea behind this was that in order to take Jerusalem and the rest of the Holy Land one should first conquer the powerful Ayyubid state in Egypt.

What followed led to one of the most spectacular feats involving ships and war techniques. Perhaps the most striking defensive feature of the riverine approach to Damietta was a tower located on an island opposite the city walls, from which there stretched a bridge of boats and a giant iron chain designed to bar traffic on the Nile (Sterling 2003, 116; Groussett 2002, 241). A first attempt to capture the tower was made by joining two ships that carried scaling ladders and a third ship equipped with a small elevated 'castle' (possibly the forerunner of the forecastle), while a trebuchet hurled stones at the walls (Figure 36). This was prepared by the Duke of Austria and the Hospitallers (Sterling 2003).

However, the attempt failed, because the depth of the river prevented a close approach to the tower, and the topography around the city made it impossible to besiege it and starve out the inhabitants. Undermining the walls was also impossible because of rough water (Sterling 2003, 117).

These conditions required a novel solution. A floating siege tower was created by lashing two ships together, and then raising four masts and four sail yards, supporting a strong 'castle' joined with poles and a network fortification (Sterling 2003).[68] The whole contraption had to be towed upstream by boats and moored against the northern wall of the tower (Sterling 2003, 118). This invention succeeded, the battle was finally won, the chain was destroyed, and the Crusaders were able to sail up the river to Damietta.

Mooring, Anchoring Landing or Beaching

At the beginning or the end of any voyage, contact has to be established between the vessel and the land. This can obviously be done in one of many ways: in a bay, a harbour, alongside a pier, or quay in a port, or simply by landing on a beach. In some cases troops, merchandise and equipment can be transported directly to a quay, or in the case of a ship anchoring off shore or off the pier, with the assistance of lighters or small boats. Animals, mainly horses in our case, apparently had to be loaded or unloaded at a pier, or directly on the beach, as described below. It is difficult to imagine how a horse weighing 500 to 1000 kg, and which would naturally be nervous and difficult to handle, could be manhandled from a ship to a lighter, or even a large skiff, although there is some evidence to the contrary, since, according to Joinville, he managed to transport eight horses to his small ship, 'petite nef' (Joinville 1995, 237).

Landing from the stern of the ship, with a door or gate opening to form a ramp, was probably more convenient than landing from the side, especially so if horses were to be landed.

The landing at Constantinople in order to conquer the city was described by Robert of Clari as follows:

As soon as they (the ships carrying the knights) had made land, the knights issued forth from the transports on their horses; for the transports were made in such a way that there was a door that could be opened and a bridge thrust out by which the knights could come out and land all mounted. (Clari 1996, 68)

Horses could, perhaps have been transported for relatively short distances in open or semi-open boats, as shown in the Bayeux Tapestry, and could simply jump off the boat. But it is difficult to see how horses could be transported across the Mediterranean, and then landed on beaches, especially if carrying knights in full armour, unless special landing doors and ramps were installed at the stern.

When landing in order to disembark troops and mounted knights from the stern opening, a ship had to approach the beach stern first. This could be done with difficulty, but without assistance if the wind was blowing directly onshore. The technique would be to sail bow-on toward the beach, estimate the distance of approximately five times the length of the vessel from the beach (depending on the steepness of the beach), drop an anchor or anchors, and then let the wind turn the ship around like a weather-vane toward the beach, allowing as much anchor cable as necessary until the vessel was safely beached. This could obviously be done if the sea bottom was sandy, or consisted of mud, and had a relatively mild slope. It could not be performed on a rocky beach.

However, if the wind was blowing off the beach, or parallel to it, such a manoeuvre would not be possible. A ship attempting to make a landing would drop an anchor at a reasonable distance from the shore, and then have her boats pull her into position with the stern toward the beach, or else land people on the beach by means of small boats and haul the ship ashore with ropes. This could not be done without using rowing boats (or at least, in some cases, a strong swimmer)

---

[68] Although a tower mounted on a Pisan ship was used against the defenders during the battle of Acre.

Chapter 5

Ports of the Holy Land and Resulting Influence on Choice of Ships

Landing on the Coast of the Holy Land

In order to try and visualize how the Crusaders managed to cope with the problems of loading and unloading along the coast of the Holy Land, we shall try to make a list of the various places known as ports, or areas suitable for anchoring, with a brief description of the characteristics of each such place.

It should be noted that even as recently as the nineteenth century the whole Syrian coast, including the Holy Land/Palestine, was considered unhealthy by seamen, as was aptly described by a British naval officer:

> The most frequented ports and trading places are, the unhealthy and dilapidated Iskanderun; Swaidiyah on the Nahr-el-A`si (Orontes); Lataki (Laodicea ad Mare); the fair town of Tarabulus (Tripolis), or Tripoli, in the East; Beirut (Berytus); Saida (Sidon); Sur (Tyr); Akka or Acre (Ptolemais); Kaipha, under Mount Carmel; Kaissariyah (Caesaria), a tolerable anchorage under a heap of ruins; Jaffa (Joppa), the port of the Western pilgrims of the Holy Land; Scalona [Ascalon] and Ghazza [Gaza], which is backed by very fertile grounds. These places are resorted to by small craft only, in the fine season, for the whole is a dreaded lee-shore in Westerly gales. (Smyth 1854, 84)

The usual ports of embarkation and disembarkation in the Holy Land were Acre and Jaffa, although Jaffa was not really a port in the true sense of the word, but just a mooring basin, poorly protected by a chain of reefs and Andromeda's Rock, with a dangerous entrance (Mirkin 2010; Mirkin 2017, 128). In any event, most of the Italian merchants were not attracted to Jaffa. The more attractive cities for merchants were Tyre, Antioch, Tripoli, and, during certain periods, Acre (Prawer 1985, 103, 183). Merchants also sailed to Alexandria in Egypt.[69] An obvious route to arrive at the Holy Land was to sail from Europe to Cyprus, from there to the coast around Tripoli or Beirut, and then down the coast to Acre or Jaffa, since this shortens the open sea passages out of sight of land.

As far as the Holy Land itself was concerned, the number of real ports, capable of offering shelter, landing piers and services was minimal, if there were any at all – except for Acre, which also had its limitations.

Port of Acre (Akko)

Acre was an important port, and during the Crusader period, was the country's major port (Galili et al., 2010, 205). In one of the books dedicated to Venetian commercial documents (Morozzo della Rocca and Lombardo 1940) Acre appears approximately 100 times under various names: Acri, Acchon, Accaron, Accharon, Accon, Acon and Acre, depending on the document's author. The documents include requests for transporting merchandise to Acre only, to Acre and Tyre, or vice versa, bills of maritime exchange, documents pertaining to property in Acre, and so forth.

The importance of the port of Acre to the Venetians is further illustrated by the fact that 30 to 40 anchors delivered by the state arsenal in Venice were transferred to Acre in August 1288 to be leased in case of bad weather to Venetian ship operators (Jacoby 2007b, 405), 'A Venetian Sailing to Acre in 1282…'). Some of the profit-yielding ventures involving commerce with or to Acre were carried out by state-owned *naves*, actually competing with private enterprise, which shows the crucial importance of Acre within Venice's trading network (Jacoby 2007b).

Many researchers think that the western basin had silted up by Crusader times; therefore ships with deeper draught had to anchor in the eastern basin, or further out in the bay (Galili et al. 2010; Gertwagen 2002, 114).

Various translations or interpretations of the original text of William of Tyre may have caused confusion as to the nature of the western or 'inner' harbour of Acre, leading to the understanding that the port was within the city walls. Researchers were, therefore, looking for a harbour within the city walls, for example, near the location of the arsenal in the old city.

However, the Latin text of William of Tyre reads as follows:

> Portum habens infra moenia et exterius, ubi tranquillam possit navibus praebere stationem. (Guillaume de Tyr, Guizot 1824, Liber Decimus, Caput XXVI)

The English version of the same text is: 'Its double port, lying both inside and outside the walls, offers a safe and tranquil anchorage to ships.' (William of Tyre 1976, Vol. I, 453)

The French translation of William of Tyre's text is slightly different, speaking about Acre or, rather, about Ptolemais, it says: 'Elle a en dedans et en dehors de ses murailles un port, dans lequel les vaisseaux trouvent une station commode et

---

[69] In later times, in the nineteenth and early twentieth centuries, most ships that went to Jaffa first sailed to Alexandria. Sailing to the Holy Land via Alexandria was also a route for fifteenth-century Jewish pilgrims, such as Meshoulam of Voltera (Eisenstein 1926, 89).

Figure 37. Acre, 4 January 1945. The right arrow points to the Tower of Flies; The left arrow points to the remnants of the watchtower (Courtesy Survey of Israel)

tranquille.' (Guillaume de Tyr, Guizot 1824, Livre Dixième, Chapitre XXVI)[70]

It seems, therefore that the French translation which speaks of 'ses murailles,' 'Its walls,' or the English version, which refers to the port as 'inside…the walls' may have led researchers to mistakenly assume the existence of a harbour within the city walls.

Moreover, one may presume that if Guillaume of Tyre had wanted to refer to the walls of the city, he would have written **eius** moenia. It may therefore be reasonable to argue that when Guillaume of Tyre referred to a port between the walls he meant between the walls of the breakwater. This is further supported by the fact that the entrance to the interior port was made between two watchtowers, one the Tower of Flies and the other at the end of the western breakwater, the remnants of which can still be seen in a photograph made by the German air force, in 1918, or, later, by the RAF.[71]

Another, more contemporary view (Figure 38) shows the suggested layout of the Acre port and its protective chains.

Remnants of a thirteenth-century wooden pier located under water, beyond the location of the western watch tower, may confirm the suggestion that there was no access to the inner harbour for deep-draught vessels, and that ships had to be anchored in the bay and could not use the quay, if such existed. The wooden pier also constituted a kind of island, not directly attached to the mainland. All this meant that loading and unloading had to be carried out by means of small boats or lighters, or, in the case of horses, by trying to beach the ships stern-on to the northern sandy shore, approximately at the present location of the Nautical School, also known as Hof Hasusim.[72]

The red circles are the probable locations of the western watchtowers, still visible on aerial photographs taken at

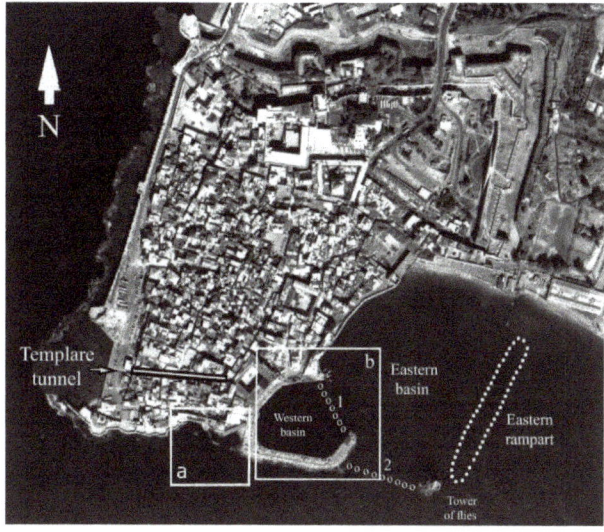

Figure 38. A – Seafront of the Pisan Quarter. B – Western basin. 1, 2 – supposed location of chains (Galili et al, 2010)

the beginning of the twentieth century, and of the eastern watchtower located on the Isle of Flies. The blue ellipse marks the approximate location where an assortment of Crusader ceramic bowls, as well as an encrusted horseshoe and animal bones, were found underwater by Prof. Michal Artzy in 2012 (Artzy 2012-2013, 12). The sandy shore is the grey area in the top right corner above the green line.[73]

In conclusion it seems that even the port of Acre, which was the best, and, actually, the only real port of the Holy Land, was not adapted to handling of cargoes such as horses, which required access to piers, and that these were probably landed by beaching the horse-bearing *huissiers* on the northern beach of the Bay of Acre, as shown in Figure 39.

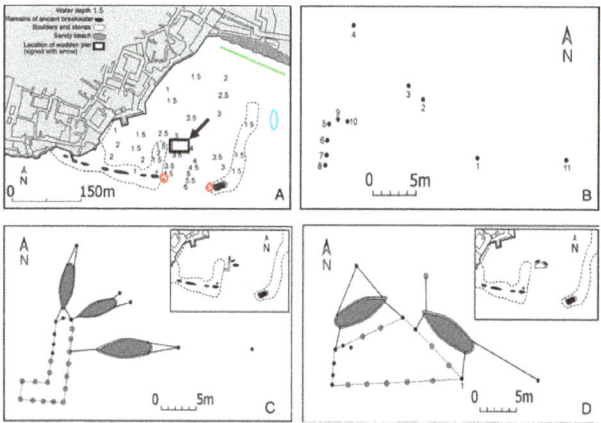

Figure 39. Acre. A – Location of the thirteenth century wooden pier. B – Location of pier's wooden columns, C and D possible reconstructions of the wooden pier and of moorings (Galili et al. 2010, 202)

---

[70] During the time of great sailing ships *vaisseau* in French meant 'ship of the line' – a great ship. Such ships did not exist during the Middle Ages.
[71] RAF: British Royal Air Force.
[72] Beach of the Horses, apparently so named because local inhabitants used to wash their horses there.

[73] The original drawing is from Ehud Galili et al. 2010. The coloured markings were added by the author.

Other Ports and Anchorages along the Coast

Atlit

South from Acre, the next point to be discussed, omitting Haifa Bay which was not a port, is Atlit. Known to the Crusaders as Château Pèlerin, Atlit had two ports: The important one was the Phoenician port in the northern bay of Atlit (Raban and Linder 1992; Haggi 2007). The other port was located adjacent to the southern side of the Crusader castle and is known as the Crusader mole. It is difficult to understand why the Crusaders chose to create a mole on the southern side, considering that the prevailing storms along this coast usually come from the southwest. In any event, no significant finds of Crusader shipping were found in the Phoenician harbour of Atlit. We found no written reports of items discovered in near the Crusader mole. According to interviews with military divers from the Atlit naval base, many ancient stone anchors were found near the Crusader mole, which conform to finds from the Phoenician harbour (Raban 1995–1956). However, proper research cannot be undertaken because Atlit is an active naval base.

Dor

Dor, approximately 8 km south of Atlit, was probably not used by the Crusaders as a port, although they built a fortress there, the remnants of which were still very much in evidence in the nineteenth century (Wilson 1881, 105). A number of wrecks were discovered in the lagoon of Dor, but none was related to the Crusaders (Wachsmann and Raveh 1984, 233–241. See also Kahanov 2011).

Caesarea

The Herodian port of Caesarea, about 10 km south of Dor, was built between 22 and 10 BCE. It had been gradually sinking and was virtually destroyed by an earthquake in around 128 CE. Attempts to repair the port carried in the Late Roman era and during the Crusader period were not successful (Raban 1992 1385–1391). Substantial buildings and fortifications were erected in Caesarea after its conquest by the King Baldwin I in 1102, and it was further fortified by Louis IX, beginning in 1251. However, despite the importance of the port in antiquity, we found no indication of use by the Crusaders of Caesarea's port, or what was left of it.

Apollonia-Arsuf

The so-called 'Apollonia Port' or 'Military Harbour' is located at the foot of the Apollonia-Arsuf Crusader castle, about two nautical miles north of the modern city of Herzliya, 30 km south of Caesarea. The enclosed basin of Apollonia-Arsuf, which will be discussed in detail below, was most probably used in some way by the inhabitants of the castle. However, ships larger than small oared craft could not enter the basin.

Jaffa

Jaffa was considered the port of Jerusalem since very early times, when the King of Tyre told King Solomon: 'And we will cut wood out of Lebanon, as much as thou shalt need: and we will bring it to thee in floats by sea to Joppa; and thou shalt carry it up to Jerusalem.' (2 Chronicles 2:16)

Richard the Lionheart landed in Jaffa in 1192, as described above. Pilgrims to the Holy Land embarked or disembarked in Jaffa, although it lacked accessible quays and was hardly, if at all, protected by reefs, among them Andromeda's Rock (Mirkin and Goren 2012, 135).

Yavne Yam

The next anchorage, approximately 20 km south of Jaffa: Yavne Yam or Yavne Maritima, is a slightly protected inlet, somewhat less than a cove, located between a cliff and *kurkar* reefs, which afford some protection. Many artifacts were discovered during underwater surveys, among them, three-holed stone anchors, which contained remnants of the wooden spikes or wedges used in such anchors. Some of these were dated to the tenth–thirteenth centuries – the Crusader era (Galili and Sharvit 2005, 308).

Figure 40a. The southern bay in Atlit and the Crusader mole. Courtesy Israel Antiquities Authority

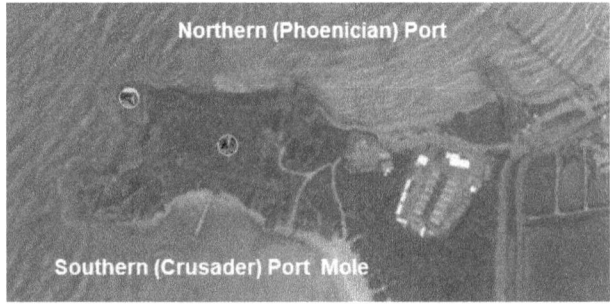

Figure 40b. Aerial view of Atlit bay, from Google Earth

Ascalon

Another very important maritime city (now known as Ashkelon), but without any real port to speak of, Aptly described by William of Tyre:

'Ascalon derives no advantage from being situated on the seacoast, for it offers no port or safe harbour for ships. It has a mere sandy beach and the violent winds make the sea around the city exceedingly choppy so that, unless the sea be calm, those who come there are very suspicious of it.' (William of Tyre, ch.6)

Even Ambroise describes the difficulty of handling ships near 'Escalone'

> Escalone siet sor la mer
> De Grece, issi l'on nomer,
> N'onques ne vi a me devise
> Nesune citié mielz assise,
> S'il eust port ou entree,
> Car trop i ad bonne contree;
> Mais la mer est si turmentuse
> Llloc endreit e perilluse
> Que nuls veissels n'i puet durer;
> E por ço covint endure
> La a noz genz tel mesestance
> Que onques uit jorz sanz dotance
> Par mer n'i pot veissel venir
> De vitaille a lost sustenir,
> Ne onques de rien n'i gusterent.
> (Ambroise 7897–7911)[74]

Although without a port or harbour, the connection to the sea played a very important role in Ascalon. One of the four gates of the city was called the Sea Gate, 'because the citizens can pass through it to the sea.' (William of Tyre, ch.6)

Hence, when Baldwin III laid siege to the city, on 25 January 1153 (Grousset 1934, vol. 2, 339). It was extremely important to extend the siege to the sea as well:

> The Lord Gerard of Sidon, one of the leading barons of the kingdom, commanded the fleet of fifteen beaked ships which were ready to sail, so that they could blockade the city by sea and both prevent those who wished to enter from getting in and also stop those who wished to leave from getting out. (William of Tyre, ch.6)

Reinforcements, a mixture of pilgrims and military men arrived at Ascalon:

> About Easter time the usual passage arrived, which brought in a crowd of pilgrims. A council was held and men were sent from the army to forbid the sailors and pilgrims, on royal authority, to return. They promised them pay and invited them all to participate in the siege and in the work which was so acceptable to God. They also brought ships, both large and small. Thus it happened that quickly, within a few days, because of a good wind, all the ships which had come over on the passage appeared before the city and a tremendous host of pilgrims, both knights and sergeants, joined our expedition. (William of Tyre, ch.6)

Passages like this show once again that the Crusaders managed to conduct naval operations along the coasts of the Holy Land without having recourse to ports, harbours, wharfs or piers, and developed the necessary techniques for loading and unloading equipment, troops, and sometimes horses.

Landing on Beaches

As described above, port facilities were not available along the coast of the Holy Land, except in Acre, where also during the Crusader period, only a limited number of ships could be moored to a wharf, if at all. This will be discussed further below.

Side (Quarter) or Stern Doors?

There exists some discussion as to the location of the gates or doors used for embarkation and disembarkation of troops and horses: Was the door or the gate located in the side, on the quarter, or the stern, or even, as was suggested by Bonino, near the bow?

While discussing this question, reference is again made to the question of landing, discussed above, since there is a close relationship between these two subjects.

Figure 41. Crusader transport ship (detail), originally part of floor mosaic (1224). Displayed on wall, San Giovanni Evangelista, Ravenna (Drawing courtesy Prof. M. Bonino)

---

[74] Now Ascalon lies on the sea/Of Greece. Thus was it named to me./ I never saw a town located/ Fairer, or better situated,/ If only it had port or entry,/ For round about is all good country;/ But the water is so perilous/ At that point, so tempestuous,/ That no vessel could ride secure/ Therein. Our men must needs endure/ Therefore hardship and suffering,/ Because no ship could come and bring/ Supplies and food into the place. (Translation: Merton Jerome Hubert).

According to Martin (2001, 244) Bonino[75] has interpreted the three vertical and two horizontal lines forming the rectangular feature at the bow (Figure 41) as a horse port and the uprights at the stern as supports for the yard when lowered. Yet, says Martin, the bow seems an unlikely position for cutting a door in the hull.

Indeed, the bow is an unlikely place for creating an opening in the ship, but the quarter also seems a less favourable position for cutting a door, unless the ship can be moored, loaded and unloaded alongside a wharf, which is not the situation along the coasts of the Levant, and especially not along the shore of the Holy Land.

If the loading, and more so, the unloading, is made through a side opening then the ship has to be beached parallel to the shoreline, with its side to the sea. It would then be much more vulnerable to waves and surf. Additionally, if the ship is beached stern-on (or even bow-on), there is a chance that only one end would be buried in the sand, and the other end would remain in deeper water. This obviously depends on the configuration of the shore, and how close to the shore the water deepens. But, if the ship is beached alongside the shore, it will necessarily touch bottom along its whole underbody, and be more difficult to sail back into the sea once the operation is finished.

Martin writes that the openings for discharging horses were probably located in the side of the ships:

> In their accounts of Crusades (1248–1254), both Villehardouin and Joinville indicate that horse ports on their particular transports were at the side of the ships (probably at the quarters). Joinville details the departure of St Louis and his men on *neis*, sailed round-ships. (Martin 2002, 241)

In reaching this conclusion Martin relied on the translation of Joinville and Villehardouin by Shaw, whom she quotes:

> We went aboard our ship at the port of Marseilles in the month of August (1248). On the day we embarked the door on the port[76] side of the ship was opened, so that all the horses we wanted to take with us oversea could be put into the hold. As soon as they were inside, the door was closed and carefully caulked, as is done with a cask before plunging it into the water, because, once the ship is on the high seas, that door is completely submerged. (Joinville, trans. Shaw 1970, 196)[77]

Martin seems to have relied on a translation error by Shaw. The original text, in ancient French, from which Shaw probably derived his translation, reads as follows:

> Au mois d'aoust entrames en nos nez a la Roche de Marseille. A celle journee que nous entrames en nos nez fist l'un ouvrir la **porte** de la nef et mist l'en touz nos chevaus ens que nous devions mener outre mer, et puis reclost l'en la **porte** et l'emboucha l'en bien aussi comme l'en naye un tonnel, pour ce quant la ne fest en la grant mer toute la porte est en l'yaue. (Joinville 1995, 220)[78]

It seems, therefore that the use of the French word 'porte' for door caused Shaw to confuse '**porte**' in French and the **port side** of the boat, thus misleading Martin.

Martin was once again misled by Shaw who translated Villehardouin as follows:

> The trumpets sounded. Each transport was attached by a tow-rope to a galley, so as to reach the other side more easily . . . The knights disembarked from the transports; they leapt into the sea up to their waists, fully armed, with helmets laced and lances in hand. In like manner our good archers, sergeants, and crossbowmen, each in his company, landed as soon as their ship touched ground . . . The sailors now began to open the doors **at the side** of the transports and lead out the horses. The knights mounted quickly, while the divisions began to draw up in due order.[79] (Villehardouin, trans. Shaw 1970, 66)

However, the original text of Villehardouin (in modern French), does not speak at all about doors at the side of the transports:

> On sonna les trompettes; et chaque galère est liée a un huissier pour passer outre plus facilement …les chevaliers sortirent des huissiers; et ils sautèrent dans la mer jusqu'a la ceinture, tout armés, les heaumes lacés et la lance à la main; et les bons archers aussi et les bons sergents, et les bons arbaletiérs, chacun avec sa compagnie, là ou elle aborda…Alors **les mariniers commencent a ouvrir les portes des huissiers, et a jeter les pons dehors**; et on commence à tirer les chevaux; et les chevaliers commencent à monter sur leurs chevaux; et les corps de bataille commencent à se ranger. (Villehardouin 1870, 53–54)

No mention at all is made whether the knights disembarked and the horses were pulled out (rather than 'led' out, as in the translation) from one of the sides or from the stern. However, mention is made of 'bridges' ('*pons*' – '*ponts*' in contemporary French) that were launched. It is probably more convenient to launch a bridge from the stern than from the side or quarter of a ship, especially when horses are concerned, since a side door would hardly be installed at sea level, but rather at the level of an upper deck, whereas a stern opening would probably have its bottom part somewhere at the waterline, when, as Joinville describes, it was 'sealed as a barrel.' It seems, therefore, that Martin may have again

---

[75] In Martin's (2002) bibliography: Bonino 1978, Lateen-rigged medieval ships. New evidence from wrecks in the Po Delta (Italy) and notes on pictorial and other documents. *IJNA*, 7.1, 9–28, 12.
[76] Emphasis by the author.
[77] In Martin's bibliography: Shaw, M. R. B. (trans.) 1970, *Chronicles of the Crusades*. New York.

[78] Emphasis by the author.
[79] Emphasis by the author.

been misled by Shaw's translation of Villehardouin (Martin 2002, 241).

It is also interesting to note the preparation of the ships and of the towing galleys before landing:

> …les chevaliers furent tous sur les huissiers avec leurs destriers; et ils furent tout armés, les heaumes lacés, et les chevaux couverts et sellés. Et les galères furent tout armées et préparées.[80] (Villehardouin 1870)

It seems that the galleys that towed the *huissiers* – the transport ships with the opening (*huis*) – gave cover to the knights who alighted from the transports, before they mounted their chargers.

When discussing the disembarkation via a stern or a side opening it would be helpful to re-examine Joinville's statement, according to which when the ship sails the whole door is submerged. This led to a debate between Pryor and Fourquin, as reflected in Martin's article (Martin 2002, 241). Fourquin wrote that as an ex-captain of a roll-on roll-off ship, he would never go to sea with the door sill underwater, even in a modern ship. Pryor countered by saying that what Joinville meant was that 'they were hit by following seas and perhaps submerged somewhat when the ship heeled' (Pryor 1982b, 390).

This question can be resolved in two ways, one from the point of view of seamanship, and the other by pure logic. As far as seamanship is concerned, every sailor knows that when a boat sails, the stern has a tendency to settle somewhat. Thus, the door or gate constructed in the stern, while above the waterline, or nearly so, when the ship is being loaded, may become partly submerged when the ship sails, and even wholly submerged for short periods, when a following sea breaks on the poop. As opposed to Pryor's argument, if the door is located in the stern some heeling would hardly affect it since it remains on the center-line of the vessel. If the door is in the side, or the quarter, then if the vessel heels to the side where the door is located, it would be partly or wholly submerged.

But simple logic would prove that the door could not be wholly submerged all the time while sailing, since, in such a case, the door would be at least partly submerged, or nearly wholly submerged while loading or discharging as well, which would render those operations impossible. One cannot load or unload, and certainly one cannot caulk a door even if it is only partly submerged. If a stern-opening door were high enough to accommodate a knight on his horse (2.25 m, Pryor 1982a, 106), it would actually cover the whole or a substantial part of the stern. If it were totally submerged at sea, it could not rise above sea level while in port. This also stems from Pryor's reply to Fourquin's note (Pryor 1982c, 390).

Joinville's description may have been somewhat exaggerated, typical of a landlubber describing fearsome maritime matters.

It seems, therefore, that the preferred landing craft would have been a shallow-draft, oar-propelled *taride* about 18 *canne* long and 14 *palmi* wide[81] at the waterline.[82] The draft, according to a reconstructed drawing (Pryor 1982b, 117–118) would be about 3 *palmi*. This corresponds to a length of 37.73 m by 3.54 m wide at the floor level of the ship, which is usually slightly below the water level, and which is therefore slightly less than the dimensions at the waterline. The draft of the *tarida* is estimated at 78 cm. However, all the Angevin texts specify that ships ordered by Charles I of Anjou, King of Sicily, should have stern-opening doors. If the ships were not equipped with stern-opening doors then troops would have to alight from a side-opening door, jump overboard, or be transported by small boats, unless the ship was moored near a wharf.

It is well known that not only oar-propelled *tarides* were used for transporting horses. Contracts signed between Louis IX and Venice called for supply of large ships, sometimes huge ones. Pryor estimates that 15 ships could carry…no more than 1,450 complete knights' entourages, i.e. 1450 horses and the same number of knights, 2,900 attendants and 1,450 grooms: a total of 1,450 horses and 5,800 Crusaders (Pryor 1982a, 108). This means slightly fewer than 100 horses per vessel.

However, *tarides* were not always oared, and some relied only on sails, and had to be towed when the wind was lacking, or near the shore (see Conquest of Majorca, above). In the *Lliber dels Fets* of James of Aragon we read the following description: 'E Don Rodrigo Liçana feu noliejar una taride daqeles que hauia estades al passage de Maylorques…E la taride era bona per adur los cauals…' (*Llibre des Fets*, 153, section 104)[83]

Assuming that this was the same kind of *taride* as those that were towed, one could deduce that in medieval Europe there existed two kinds of *tarides* capable of carrying horses: one that used sails and, when necessary, oars, and one that relied on sails only.

Huissiers were not only oared *tarides*, but also sailing transport ships equipped with openings to allow unloading of horses. However, being sailing ships not propelled by oars, sometimes they needed to be towed. Villehardouin specifically writes that they were attached to galleys and towed in order to reach 'the other side': 'et chaque galère est liée a un huissier pour passer outre plus facilement.'

---

[80] 'The knights were all on the *huissiers* with their chargers; and they were all armed, and the helmets laced, and the horses covered and saddled. And the galleys were all armed and readied.'

[81] Approximately 3.6 m wide by 37.8 m long.
[82] An average taken from texts extracted from the Angevin archives, cited by Pryor 1982, 114–115.
[83] And Don Rodrigo Lizana chartered one of the tarides that had taken part in crossing to Majorca,… and the *taride* was good for carrying the horses. (Translation from Catalan, Smith and Buffrey, 120).

Sailing to the Holy Land

On the other hand, oared *tarides* need not be towed. They had sails that enabled them to tackle long distances, but also oars that enabled them to manoeuvre. Also, shallow *tarides* (approximately 76 cm draft), could approach the beach more closely, so the knights would not need to be submerged up to their belts in water when jumping off the ship. However, not only shallow-draught *tarides*, but also stern-opening sailing transport ships, which were probably some kind of a round ship, like the one illustrated in the mosaic in San Giovanni Evangelista, Ravenna, participated in landings in general, and in the landing described by Villehardouin in particular. Such ships indeed required the assistance of oared galleys in order to turn around and approach the beach stern-on, but probably could not approach the shore too closely due to their deeper draught.[84]

Another kind of horse-carrying craft is the *sallandrum* or *salandria* built by the Genovese shipwrights for Louis IX, each to carry 100 *destriers*[85] (Macintosh and Steinmayer, 1999, 114)

How to Get off the Beach

Landing troops is only part of the problem. Once the soldiers, knights, grooms, horses and equipment were landed, ships had to be returned to the sea, either without the troops, or with them or, at least, with those that had survived. This would not constitute a major problem in the Atlantic or the English Channel, because the technique could be to land on the beach just before the ebb (low tide) and get off at high tide. In the Mediterranean most of the time the tides are not significant; they vary around 8–15 cm between low and high tide, the maximum being around 40 cm between the low low tide and high high tide,[86] at spring tide. Thus the tidal variation in the Mediterranean can help or hinder, but usually cannot be counted on to change matters radically.

In order to pull a ship off the beach one would normally try to take off any superfluous weight. Obviously, once troops, horses and weapons have alighted from the ship it draws less water, and the amount by which the ship rises can be calculated according to the TPC formula (tons per centimetre immersion). This equals, roughly, the length of the ship (in metres) at water level multiplied by the beam (in metres) at water level, multiplied by the waterplane coefficient (CWP) – the ratio between the vessel's area at water line and a rectangle of the same length and breadth as the ship – and multiplied by 0.01, in order to obtain the result in centimetres. Assuming the density of sea water is about 1000 kg per m³ the weight change to increase or decrease the draught by 1 cm is:

$L \times B \times CWP \times 0.01 =$ tons per cm, where

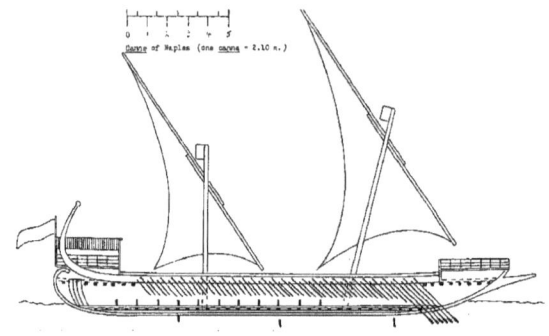

Figure 42. Longitudinal section of the *taride* built at Brindisi in 1278 for Charles I of Anjou, King of Sicily (Drawing J. H. Pryor, The Mariner's Mirror, Vol. 68 No. 1, courtesy the Society for Nautical Research)

L = length at waterline m
B = beam at waterline m

We do not have a precise plan view of a *taride* to calculate the CWP, so it can be assumed to be 0.7 for such a long narrow vessel with sharp ends (Figure 42).

The CWP of a round ship can be assumed to be 0.6.

The dimensions of a *taride* of King Charles I, at the floor (the lowest deck) were 37.73 m by 3.93 m (Pryor[b] 118).

The TPC for a *taride* is thus: $37.73 \times 3.93 \times 0.7 \times 0.01 = 1.04$ tons

This means that taking 1 ton off the *taride* would make it rise in the water by about 1 cm.

To calculate the weight of the horses that alight from a *taride*, with knights, grooms and so forth. Clari writes of 40 horses in one *huissier* (Clari 1966, 133). Marino Sanudo Torsello (2011) writes of a fleet of 24 galleys embarking 400 horses, which would make fewer than 20 horses per vessel (Pryor 1982b, 109). Various estimates are given, ranging from the fantastic: 15 ships carrying 4,000 horses (Pryor 1982a, 108), to 15 ships carrying 1,450 horses, and the 'same number of knights, 2,900 attendants and 1,450 grooms '(Pryor 1982a), which would make nearly 100 horses per ship, in addition to their equipment. A more conservative calculation would count 30 *destriers* (war horses) per ship, plus 30 knights, 30 grooms and 60 attendants. Various sources assume that the *destrier* weighed approximately 540 kg, and the knight 54 kg.[87] The armour weighed another 50 kg. Assuming that the knight, horse and armour weighed 650 kg, and multiplied by 30 (the proposed number of knights) the total equals 19 tons. Ninety attendants and grooms would add another 5 tons. Add mariners, equipment, arms, perhaps food, etc., and we arrive at approximately 25 tons. If this weight was removed, a *taride* would rise by 25 cm.

---

[84] Interestingly, ancient galleys were sometimes equipped with ladder-like gangways in the bow or stern, and some carried two landing ladders hanging off the stern (Casson 1995, 251).
[85] War horses
[86] Data from Israel Oceanographic and Limnological Research.

[87] For example: http://www.horsemanmagazine.com/2009/08/war-horses-and-medieval-knights, retrieved 28 October 2014.

With regard to a round ship, Marco Bonino's reconstruction puts the overall length at 33.2 m and the beam at 9.6 m at deck level (Martin 2001, 47). As a ship has overhangs, it is longer and wider at the deck level than at the waterline, so to arrive at the dimensions at the waterline, one has to deduct about 2 m from the overall length, and about 0.6 m from the beam. The CWP of a round ship could be assumed to be 0.6.

The TPC for a round ship is thus: $31.2 \times 9.0 \times 0.6 \times 0.01 = 1.68$ cm

Thus, removing 1.68 tons from a round ship would cause it to rise 1 cm, and removing 25 tons would cause it to rise approximately 14 cm.

Before beaching stern (or bow)-on, an expert seaman would drop an anchor a good distance off the beach. Thus the angle of the anchor cable would be as shallow as possible, and the cable as horizontal as possible in order to afford a more efficient purchase and angle of tow. The crew can then try to get the ship off by pushing by hand, and trying to use the ship's capstan if it had one, to take as much strain as possible on the anchor.

If the Greeks had capstans, and sailing galleys or other ships in the fifteenth century had them as well, one could assume that the Venetians and Genovese who supplied ships to the Crusaders also had capstans, and that these could help in pulling the ships off the beaches.

I encountered no descriptions or commissions for a capstan on the *huissiers* or *tarides*, but it is known that ancient, even Greek, sailing ships had capstans mounted near the bow (Casson 1995, 252). The fifteenth-century sailor, author and naval researcher Michael of Rhodes, in his specification for building and equipping a 'Galley of Flanders', specifies a capstan, and gives its dimensions (Michael of Rhodes 1992, vol. 2, 441). The fifteenth-century traveller Meshoulam of Volterra tells how the ship on which he travelled was nearly sunk near Alexandria, but the Genoese came from Alexandria, dropped anchors and by use of a capstan or windlass managed to save the ship (Yaari 1977, 117–118).

The conclusion I propose is that ships intended to carry Crusaders to ports known for having convenient wharfs or piers may have had side-opening doors. Those destined to sail to the Holy Land and designed to carry horses were most probably stern-opening ships.

The following figures demonstrate the difficulty of using regular gangways. These illuminations, mostly from the fourteenth and fifteenth centuries, depict people, mostly notables, such as kings, alighting from ships anchored near the shore.

In Figure 43 King Louis alights from the bow of a ship, directly to the shore. The angle of the gangway on which he walks is steep, showing that it is attached at the level of the deck, with no opening in the side.

Figure 43. *Arrivée de Louis IX à Limassol*. BnF MSS Français 2634, fol. 411 (c. 1310)

Figure 44. *Débarquement des Normands en France* (c. 1375). BnF, MS Français 2813, fol. 165

The same also applies to Normans disembarking in France (Figure 44) although, since the angle of the gangway is not so steep, one can assume that either the ship was lower, or the shore, at the foot of the castle, was somewhat higher than the level of the sea. In both cases the water is rather deep next to the shore.

Two illuminations (Figures 45 and 46) show a gangway arranged from the deck to a river bank, which acts like a wharf or pier. Again, no special arrangements or openings for disembarking are shown.

Figure 47 contains three pictures. At top right a vessel is anchored lengthwise along the shore, with two gangways at very steep angles, denoting the lack of a pier of wharf. The bottom picture could not conform to reality, because the gangway is attached to a ship with a fully billowing sail.

Sailing to the Holy Land

Figure 45. Crowning of Louis IV (left), assassination of Guillaume Longue Epée (right). BnF, MS Français 6465, fol. 159v (1455?)

Figure 47. Romance of Destruction of Troy (late fifteenth century). Bodleian Library Douce MS 353, fol. 31

Figure 46. The Naval Battle of Cadsand. BnF Français MS 2643 fol. 42v

According to the state of the sea and the sail the wind is quite strong, so the only explanation might be that the ship was depicted sailing away in haste; a figure in a small boat made fast to the ship seems hurriedly trying to climb on board, In such a situation, the gangway would subsequently fall into the water and be left behind.

Thus it can be concluded that if there were no horses to unload, but rather only troops, no special openings were made in the vessels, at the stern or in the side, and sailors often arrived side-on to the beach, bank or shore, relying on the possibility of refloating the ship and bringing it back out to the sea.

Figure 48. Richard II meeting with rebels (fifteenth century). BnF, MS 2644, fol. 154v

Figure 48 shows a boat approaching the shore without any arrangements for landing (or perhaps to prevent the rebels on the shore from boarding). The boat lacks masts and sails, and is therefore probably some kind of a river boat or, more probably, the Royal Barge, propelled by oars. If there is no need to unload horses – no special openings should be incorporated in the vessel.

PART 2

APOLLONIA-ARSUF: A MARITIME INSTALLATION BELOW THE CASTLE

Chapter 6

General Description and Research Project

Apollonia-Arsuf in the Crusader Period

On 7 June 1091 Richard the Lionheart sailed with 25 ships from Tyre to Acre. This was only part of his fleet: most of his transports, carrying many barons, their entourages and much of his siege equipment, were detained in Tyre because of adverse winds (Gillingham 1999, 159).

> Ambroise describes this:
> E li manda que son barnage
> Ne s'estoire n'iert pas venu,
> Einz l'aveit uns tens detenu,
> Que l'em claime li venz d'Arsur,
> E l'avait arrestee a Sur.
> (Ambroise 4610–4615)[88]

Ambroise called this adverse wind 'the wind of Arsur',[89] rather than referring to it as a strong wind, or a 'vent contraire' (Ambroise 11016). The fact that he described the southern wind as 'the wind of Arsur' proves the importance of this site, as either a fortress, a town, or perhaps an important maritime location.

The so-called port or military harbour of Apollonia is located at the foot of the cliff on which the Crusader castle stands, about 2 nautical miles north of the modern city of Herzliya. This built installation is trapezoidal, measuring about 80 m from north to south and 33 m from east to west. It has walls[90] at its northern and southern sides, and the western side is protected by a *kurkar* ridge with a signs of a destroyed structure on the top. There were round structures (watchtowers?) at the seaward ends of the walls, and there may have been an entrance at its southwestern corner.

Figure 50, from the mid-twentieth century, as well as a recent GIS, give us an idea of the appearance of the watchtowers before their destruction.

A detailed view of the remnants of the northern watchtower, and part of the northern wall can be seen in the GIS (Figure 51).

Opinions differ as to the true nature of the site, and whether it was a real port or harbour.[91] Was it just a mooring basin for small craft? Or, as some scholars claim, was it just an installation designed to prevent an approach from the coast to the cliff on which the castle itself stood? The field work described here was carried out within the port itself as well as in the deeper waters surrounding it, attempted to elucidate these questions.

Apollonia, or as it was called in medieval times, Arsuf or Arsur, is frequently mentioned with reference to the various Crusades. One of the better-known references is to the Battle of Arsuf, in the Third Crusade, in which Richard I

Figure 49. Aerial view of the Apollonia-Arsuf port today. The blue arrows indicate the walls (breakwaters?) and the red arrow – the remnants of the northern watchtower

Figure 50. Remnants of the southern watchtower, 1953 (Central Zionist Archive)

---

[88] 'He sent word thereof to the King/ And that fleet, which was to bring/ His barons to him still remained/ At Tyre, because it was detained/ By what is called the Arsur wind.' (Translation: Merton Jerome Hubert)
[89] Arsur is another medieval name for Apollonia-Arsuf.
[90] These walls actually act as breakwater, whether this installation was meant to be a port, or just an installation designed to protect the cliff.
[91] For convenience this maritime installation is further referred to as 'the port'. This, however, should not be deemed as confirmation that this installation was a port.

Sailing to the Holy Land

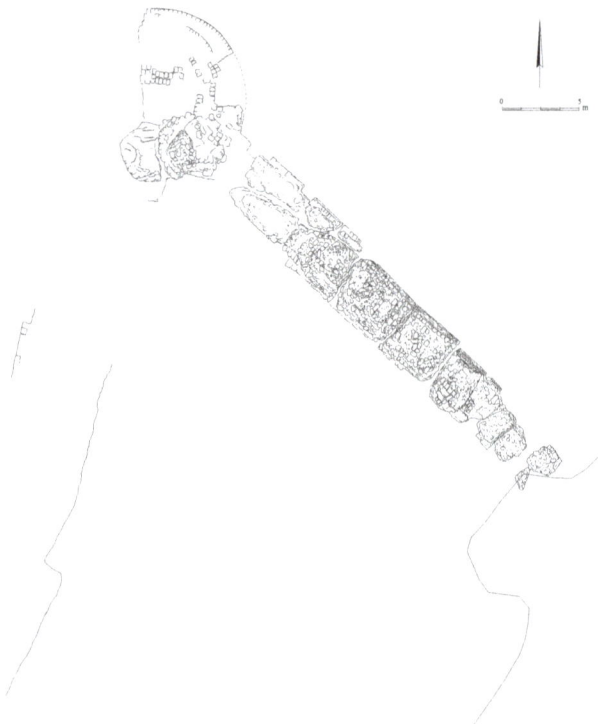

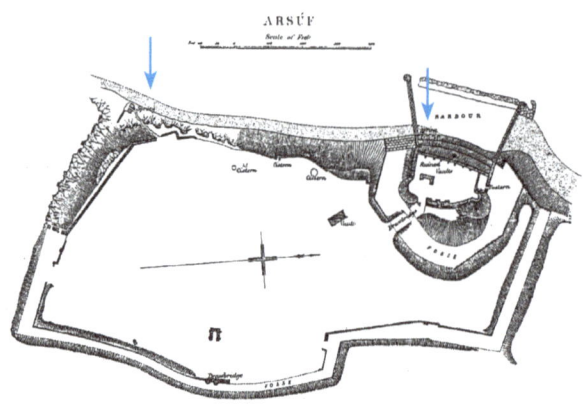

Figure 51. GIS of part of the base of the northern watchtower and part of the northern wall

of England (Richard the Lionheart) defeated Saladin on 7 September 1191.

Between 1187 and 1191 the site was still under Ayyubid control; but an important Crusader town located near the sea in that area, had probably established some means of direct contact with the sea in the twelfth century, be it for logistical support or maritime communication with other entities having access to the sea.

Figure 52. Remnants of the northern watchtower (Beginning to mid 20th Century – Central Zionist Archive)

Figure 53. Survey of Arsuf, PEF. Conder C.R., Kitchener H.H., 1882-1888 'Survey of Western Palestine, Memoir Vol. II – Samaria, Sheet X Section B. opp. p. 137'. The blue arrows indicate the springs

It is well known that the Franks attempting to conquer Arsuf were assisted by Italian fleets (Asbridge 2012, 123). Indeed, as one of the main and basic problems of fleets in those days was a supply of fresh water, it can be safely assumed that Arsuf's two springs (one of them active to this day) certainly enhanced its importance and attraction to foreign fleets. One of the springs was described in the 1881 survey by the Palestine Exploration Fund[92] (Conder and Kitchener 1882, 138), and both are depicted in the drawing made by the surveyors (Figure 53).

Evidence of Use as a Maritime Installation in Crusader Times

In the middle of the last century one could still climb up from the beach to the fortress through a tunnel let into the face of the cliff. The location of the tunnel is still known, although it is now blocked by debris.[93] One may assume that inhabitants of the fortress in the mid-thirteenth century had the means to go down to the shore, and may also have used this or another direct means to get access to the shore. Ongoing excavations are still trying to locate a direct link between the castle and the shore.

It is, therefore, not surprising that, apparently, sea transport was used to communicate with the thirteenth-century castle, and probably its twelfth century predecessor. One known example refers to Baldwin I, King of Jerusalem, in the early stages of Crusader rule. He found refuge in Arsuf, after the debacle of the Battle in Ramla, in May 1102, when the King's small army of mounted knights was defeated by a superior force of Egyptian troops.

Desiring to join his troops in Jaffa, King Baldwin was picked up from Arsuf by the pirate Goderic, and managed to escape

---

[92] Palestine Exploration Fund, created 1865.
[93] Interview with Prof. Emeritus Dan Jacobson, Tel Aviv University, who says that he used to climb through the tunnel in his early teens, which was considered an act of bravado.

and avoid Egyptian ships trying to encircle Goderic's ship, referred to as a *buza*,[94] as recounted by Albert of Aix:

> Verum dehinc septem diebus evolutis, rex ab Assur exiens, navem, quae dicitur buza, ascendit, et cum eo Godericus pirata de regno Anglia.[95]

There seems to be no other evidence describing the use of Arsuf as an embarkation point. The story does not specify how Goderic entered the water off Arsuf in order to pick up King Baldwin, whether the King swam out to meet the *buza* in the open sea (which also defies imagination) or, more likely, the King, or Goderic himself, used a small boat to row out to sea and meet the ship.

The text tells us, however, that Goderic's boat was light and agile and thus managed to avoid 20 galleys and 13 barks of a type that the Saracens called *cazh* and: 'in Portu Joppe, delusis hostibus, subito adfuit'[96] (Albert of Aix. *Historia Hierosolymitanae Expeditionis,* Liber IX, ch. IX).

The Research Project

This episode spurred researchers in the Department of Archaeology in Tel-Aviv University to study the later, mid-thirteenth century, structure of the port of Arsur castle, which, if it did serve as a maritime installation, would have most likely facilitated logistics in loading and unloading people, animals and cargo alike.[97]

The 'port is trapezoidal, some 80 m long by 33 m wide, and its four corners are:

1. Northwest corner: 32°11'45.18" N; 34°48'21,12" E
2. Southwest corner: 32°11'42,45" N; 34°48'22,35" E
3. Northeast corner: 32°11'44,52" N; 34°48'22,27" E
4. Southeast corner: 32°11'42,04" N; 34°48'21,53" E

Judging by aerial photographs one suspects immediately that the walls or breakwaters surrounding the port are manmade.

The presence of such structures obviously leads to the question of their purpose. Were they built to create a mooring area? Or an installation intended to facilitate communication with vessels anchored offshore in deep water? Or perhaps, as some researchers suggest, the structure's only goal was to protect the cliff (Flemming et al., 1978).

Sub-bottom Sonar Scan

To attempt to trace maritime activity around the port, it was decided to proceed with an underwater sonar scan. Two experts were engaged to conduct underwater and ground penetrating research in the area surrounding the installation: Dr. K. Storch the inventor and longtime user of special sediment sonar, of the firm SoSo, and Dr. Hans Günter Martin, of the firm Abatonos (see Appendix A). The scans were performed between 30 September 2010 and 6 October 2010, mainly around the port, partly close to the shore, the 'Inner Area,' and in the area located more to seaward, the 'Outer Area'. Very little work could be done within the port itself, since its bottom was almost completely covered with stones and debris that had fallen from the fortress on the cliff top, and effectively blocked the penetrating capacity of the sonar.

The sediment sonar equipment used was a perpendicular bifrequential sonar. The transducer produces two signals of constant strength and the reflections were measured. This allowed under most circumstances to penetrate the sediment to a certain depth and to locate all hard finds or objects. The positioning was done by a combined DGPS.[98] All positions were given in dd.dddd (decimal points to the fourth place) in WGS 84 (World Geodetic System 84). The scanner itself was mounted on the stern of a small 'RIB' (rigid-bottom rubber dinghy) with a 10 HP Yamaha outboard motor. Electric power was supplied from a car battery. The accompanying computer was protected in a metallic box, and the additional DGPS aerial was erected on the cliff.

The dinghy was launched from the beach, often having to first cross the surf, and was usually operated by two people: Dr. Stork, who operated the sonar, and a boat driver, trying to follow a pattern of overlapping lines to cover each search area.

The primary result of the scan before being deciphered translated itself to 39 plates, such as those presented in Figures 54 and 55.

Each plate represents a different depth of penetration. When a certain phenomenon repeats itself on different plates, as, for example, indicated by the blue arrows below in Figure 55 (the yellow line of dots on the dark pink background versus the green line of dots on the yellow background), this may indicate the presence of an item that might require further investigation ('target').

---

[94] It is not clear whether the *buza* is a craft known in the Middle Ages as *buzza, bucia* or *bucius*, developed from the Viking long ships. Ray Martin refers to *buzo nave, buzus* and *buzusnavis* (Martin 2001, 175) as merchant or transport ships current in the thirteenth century.

[95] Albert of Aix, *Historia Hierosolymitanae Expeditionis,* Liber IX, ch. IX.

'After the passage of seven days, the King exited from Assur and boarded a boat called *buza*, with Godericus a pirate of the kingdom of England.'

[96] 'Having deluded or [deceived] the enemies, all of a sudden they [or 'it] '] found themselves [or 'itself] '] in the port of Jaffa ' (translation by the author).

[97] The study of the installation was pioneered by Prof. Nicholas Flemming and the late Prof. Avner Raban, who wrote: 'It is not possible to say whether this structure was a landing stage, part of the city fortifications, or a harbour basin. The last-mentioned seems unlikely in view of the small size, shallowness, and lack of entrance' (Flemming and Raban, 1978, 66). Dr. Eva Grossman investigated the installation in her Ph.D. dissertation (Grossmann, 1995) which was later published as a monograph (Grossmann 2001): Some of the finds she published, such as a three-hole anchor, also appeared elsewhere, e.g., Grossmann and Kingsley 1996.

[98] A regular GPS which uses an additional aerial emitting a signal, located at some distance from the GPS itself, and in our case, on the cliff top. This allows for more precise GPS data.

Sailing to the Holy Land

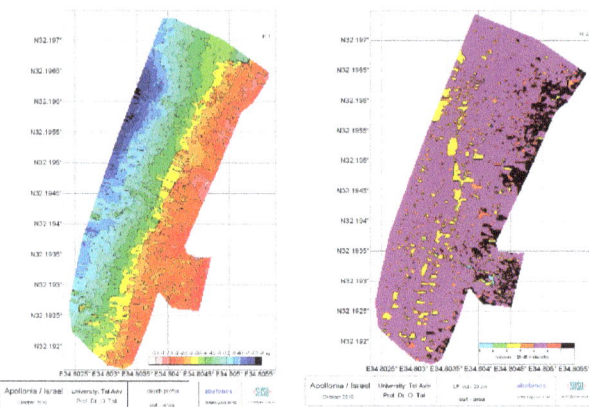

Figure 54. 'Outer Area'

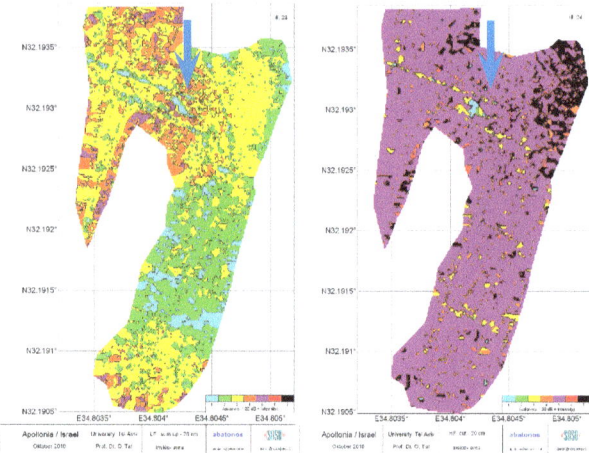

Figure 55. 'Inner Area

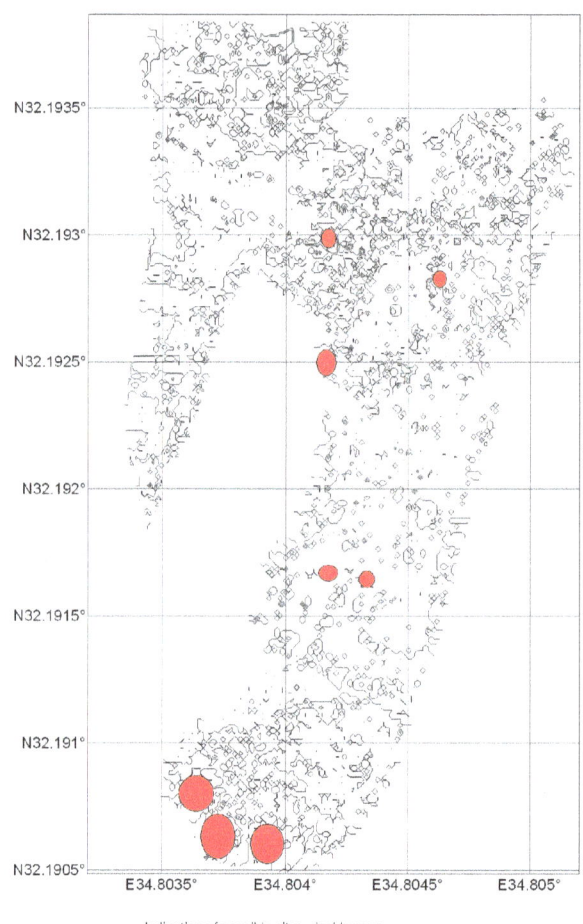

Figure 56. Targets in the 'Inner Area'

After interpreting the data, Abatonos prepared tables of possible targets as shown in Figure 56.

For the convenience of plotting on a marine chart, the coordinates of the various points were translated from the decimal system to the minutes and seconds system:[99] The possible targets were also positioned on a Google aerial photograph and numbered 'Apo 1', etc.

Water-jetting

Water-jetting involves pumping a strong jet of water penetrating vertically into the seabed to dislodge sand and any objects which may be present. It penetrates the sand, and any objects of interest located under the sand are lifted to the top of the seabed. The water jet is directed by a diver, who collects samples, which are brought up to the boat.

Water-jetting Attempt 1

19 June 2011. The equipment consisted of a boat from the Herzliya Marina, provided by the Reef Diving Club, equipped with a 75 HP Mercury motor driving a 2-inch pump connected to a 15-m long fire hose, connected in turn to a 3/4 in diameter steel pipe 3-m long. A first attempt was made to water-jet some of the targets. For various reasons the attempt failed to reveal any finds.

Water-jetting Attempt 2

11 June 2012. On board, in addition to the author, was the boat's skipper, a diver himself and three more divers. Targets were located with a GARMIN 550 GPS equipped with a camera.[100]

The points where the water jetting was carried out were identified as New 1, New 2, etc.

First point: New 1; coordinates: Lat: N 32.19060; Long:E 034.8039007.15.

Depth of water in New 1 was approximately 1.80 m. Water-jetting was carried out to the depth of 3 m through the sand down to a rocky bottom; there were no finds.

---

[99] The complete report, as received, is attached as Appendix A to the present book. The coordinates of the various targets are enclosed as Appendix B.

[100] Although plotting on marine charts is usually done using the degrees, minutes and seconds system, the readout in the GPS was converted to the decimal system to conform to the Abatonos report, and avoid conversion mistakes, using the international WGS 84 datum used by GPS.

Figure 57. Targets marked by yellow pins on Google Earth map. Green dot – piece of *Cedrus libani*; red dot – olive pit; light blue dot near Apo 10 – metal-impregnated wood ('New 3-3' in Table 2)

Second point: New 3; Lat: 32.19080 N; Long: 034.80360 E.

Depth of water: approximately 2 m. Depth of sand, approximately 4.5 m. At the depth of 3 m a non-porous piece of wood was found. More porous pieces of wood were found at a depth of 4.5 m under the sand, with what appeared to be an olive pit. A much eroded jar handle (Hellenistic?) was also found.

The exact point where the pieces of wood were found was marked in the GPS as NEW2FOUNDWOOD, and its precise location was Lat: 32.19089 N; Long: 034.80354 E.

Third point: New 9: Lat: 32.19650 N; Long: 034.80470 E.

This point is located seaward of the reef line. Depth of water approximately 5.5 m. Pieces of wood were found under 1 m of sand.

Water-jetting Attempt 3

18 June 2012

First point: Monday 2; Lat: 32.11550 N; Long: 034.48247 E.

Depth of water: 3 m. This point was very close to the reef on the seaward side of the port; a strong swell prevented possibility of work.

This was significant not only as far as water-jetting was concerned, but because it proved the difficulty that an ancient seafarer would have encountered in threading his way through a series of reefs approaching the port.

Second point: New-10; Lat: 32.11832 N; Long: 034.48234 E.

Depth of water: 5–7 m. The following finds were located on the seabed after water-jetting the sand to a depth of approximately 2.5 m: The olive pit, sharp at both ends, another item resembling an almond, and a larger pit, which looked like a peach stone, were found. In addition, some pieces of wood, including one about 8 cm long, which looked somewhat newer, were found.

Each of the finds was inserted into a small plastic bag, marked with the name of the point where it was found and numbered sequentially within that point. The name of the point was written in pencil on a piece of cardboard and inserted into the same bag. This work was supervised by Dr. Nili Liphschitz, an expert in dendroarchaeology and dendrochronology, and by the archaeologist Prof. Oren Tal. The finds were sent to the ETH Laboratory of Ion Beam Physics in Zurich, for radiocarbon dating, accompanied by a list (Appendix C).

Significant ^{14}C Results

The results of the dating which were found to be significant are listed in Table 2:

Table 2: Significant radiocarbon dating results from the 18 June water-jetting

ID No.	Site	Tree species	Calib. ETH ^{14}C (95% probability)
ETH-46902	New 3-3	*Pistacia* sp., metal impregnated	1280–1400 CE 95%
ETH-46903	New 9-1	*Cedrus libani*, A long piece	1660–1890 CE 78%
			1900–1950 CE 16.7%
ETH-46909	New 10-1	*Cupressus sempervirens*, Piece of wood	1640–1690 CE 33.7%
			1730–1810 CE 46.7%
			1930–1960 CE 15%
ETH-46910	New 10-3	Olive pit (*Olea europaea*)	880 CE–1020 CE 95.4%

The finds represent three different time periods, and might indicate the possible location of a wreck or wrecks at some of the sites.

Further water-jetting in the areas suggested in the sonar research report will be conducted in order to try and locate additional finds.

The Excavation

In order to determine whether the port could indeed have served as a harbour for sea-going vessels several questions must be answered:

- Are the entrances to the port practicable, and, if so, under what sea conditions?
- What is the depth in the port, assuming that it was free of debris and silt?
- How were the walls built? What kind of stones was used and what are their sizes?
- Was the sea level substantially different in Crusader times from the present day?

It was decided that in order to obtain at least partial answers, the port would have to be partially dredged to remove at least some of the silt, stones that had fallen from the castle and other debris, which would allow the port's depth to be ascertained. Water-jetting would have to be performed in many points to try to ascertain depths, and also to locate finds, if any, beneath the seabed.

In order to protect the cliff against erosion by the sea waves, in the winter of 2009, huge limestone boulders were placed on the narrow sandy beach, to the south and north of the ancient Port, at the foot of the castle and to its west, making approach on foot from the south extremely difficult and hazardous. As for the approach from the north, the beach cannot be accessed by vehicle, making overland transport of excavation and dredging equipment such as the water-pump, dredgers, and dive gear impossible. Hence, there was a need to find a solution to transport the equipment by sea.

The dredging pump, which weighs approximately 250 kg, was mounted on a wooden platform on a rubber boat (Figure 58), which was brought to the site from Herzliya Marina. The operation was done very early in the morning when the sea is relatively calm, because the boat, being very top-heavy, was not designed for such work and any beam wave could have capsized it. Shallow rocks at the entrance to the site required that the boat's outboard engine be raised, and it was rowed in. The rest of the equipment – air-tanks, dredgers, fire hoses, pipes, dive gear, office supplies, food, etc. – was transported on a flat-bottomed motorboat that was walked into the Port, through the narrow entrance in the reef, which forms the port's western, seaward 'wall' or breakwater (?) (Figure 59). A temporary camp was established on a small beach at the foot of the cliff. Electricity and water were brought down by long hoses and cables from Apollonia National Park, located at the top of the cliff, and a tent was erected for a guard who remained on the site during the entire operation, which lasted five days, from 3 to 7 November 2013.

Figure 59. Walking the boat in (Photo: A. Yurman)

Figure 60. Paddling out with empty air tanks (Photo: A. Yurman)

Figure 58. The dredging pump mounted on the rubber dinghy, with a diving flag, moored in the port (Photo: A. Yurman)

Except during the first stage of installation and later, when the camp was dismantled, the motorboat remained outside the reef, and air-tanks and provisions were paddled into the port on a kayak or rubber dinghy (Figure 60).

Many pieces of machinery, diving and water-jetting equipment and so forth were delivered to the camp site. For the detailed list see Appendix D.

Workforce

A notice calling for volunteer divers was published at the Universities of Tel Aviv and Haifa, as well as on the Internet, and more than 60 people applied. They were vetted by the dive-masters of the Maritime Workshop of the Leon Recanati Institute for Maritime Studies of the University of Haifa. The approximately 30 selected applicants were divided into groups, each group consisting of two or three divers, one supervisor of the dredger pump (to be able to stop it in case of emergency), and one person on shore to ensure that divers who entered the water also returned to shore. In addition, at least two people carried out the water-jetting, and one or two made drawings above or below the water.[101]

Tasks

The work was divided into two main areas: first, studying the northern and southern built walls, as well as the western wall, consisting of a natural reef with some remnants of masonry; and, second, studying the seabed. A total of 119 dives were made under the supervision of the dive-masters. The work included clearing of stones and rubble, excavation of trenches, water-jetting and documenting the constructions on the site in the attempt to understand whether they were indeed meant to act as breakwaters, protecting a harbour or landing stage, or were part of the city's fortifications.

Clearing the Seabed

The first stage mainly involved clearing stones and rubble scattered on part of seabed in the port, most of which, as noted, had fallen down from the castle over the years. This was done to create areas of clear seabed that could later be cleared of silt to measure water depth (Figure 61).

The stones, generally ashlars measuring about 40×30×25 cm, were collected into crates, dragged under water and deposited outside the northern wall. When a substantial area of the north-western part of the port was cleared of heavy rubble and stones, the excavation commenced, employing two dredgers. It was decided to first try to dredge a deep trench, in order to examine the foundation of the northern wall (or breakwater), and the western reef. When the trench reached the depth of about 1.5 m divers were instructed not to excavate under the wall so as to avoid danger of collapse. After the foundations of the wall or breakwater and of the

Figure 61. Diver clearing debris (Photo: A. Yurman)

northern watchtower were examined, it was decided to extend the trench eastward, toward the shore. At a later stage the trench was extended southward and deepened.

Because much of the area of the port was covered with large sections of the fallen castle wall, and the excavated trench proved that the bedrock was much deeper than was first realized (about 2.5 m rather than approximately 1 m) it was decided that better knowledge could be gained by water-jet probes in many areas of the site, and then measuring the depths of the seabed (Figure 62).

Seventy-four probes were carried out at 2 m intervals. Some of the probes were so deep that the probe itself, about 2.5 m long, was sunk completely into the seabed. Some probes hit

Figure 62. Water-jetting (Photo: A. Avidor)

---

[101] The work was supervised by Prof. Y. Kahanov, Dr. D. Cvikel of the University of Haifa, and by the author.

Sailing to the Holy Land

rocky bottom at a shallow depth. The probes were performed along four lines (marked in red in Figure 63).

Each water-jetting point was logged, and two figures were recorded: the upper one – the depth of the water at that particular point, and the lower figure: the depth of penetration of the probe until it hit hard bottom, rock, or, in some cases, sank its entire length into the sea-bottom without encountering resistance. (See Appendix E)

Figure 63. Water-jetting was carried out along the lines marked in red (Photo: Skyview Ltd.)

Chapter 7

Findings

The Northern and Southern Walls (Breakwaters?)

Until the present research was carried out (2013) it was believed that the site was surrounded by manmade masonry and by a natural reef (Flemming et al. 1978].). It was apparent that the northern and southern walls were artificial. The lowest layer of the stones constitutes a protruding ledge, slightly wider than the upper part of the wall (Figure 64). However, it is not certain that this protrusion was intended to be a ledge, or whether the whole construction was wider, and that part of it, above the ledge, had disappeared over the years, leaving the ledge-like wider section.[102]

The northern wall was built on a soft *kurkar* ramp (Figure 65). This may support the theory that the port was deeper than previously assumed, and that the builders found the need to create a ramp and build a stone breakwater on its upper part to withstand the waves.

Excavation of the trench eased access to the base of the northern wall. Work then proceeded with the drawing and photographing of structures, above and below water, for example, a drawing of a part of the northern wall (Figure 66), a photograph of an area close to it (Figure 67), a photograph of staircase-like part of the northern wall, from the north (Figure 68), and a photograph of the trenches indicating their depth below water level (Figure 69).

Figure 65. Headers on a ramp (Photo: A. Yurman)

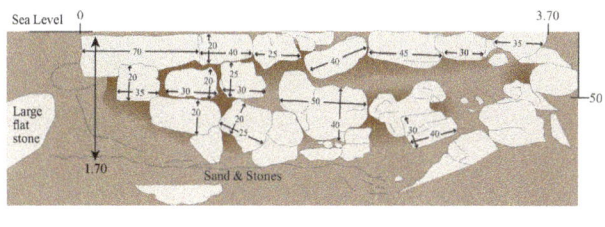

Figure 66. Western section of the northern wall (by Yaacov Assuli, after sketch by J. B. Tresman)

Figure 64. Protruding ledge (Photo: A. Yurman)

Figure 67. Western section of the northern wall (Photo: A. Yurman)

---

[102] Similar construction in larger and smaller stones is evident in the castle itself.

Sailing to the Holy Land

Figure 68. Western section of the northern wall, from the north, with staircase-like ashlars (Photo: A. Yurman)

Figure 70. Headers on a ramp acting as foundation (Photo: A. Yurman)

Figure 69. The trench at 1.2 m below water level (Photo: A. Yurman)

Figure 71. 'Clean' stones recently uncovered (Photo: A. Yurman)

At the base of the northern wall, the trench reached a depth of 2.4 m. Newly uncovered stones, which were 'clean', as opposed to the upper courses that were found covered by marine fouling (Figure 71).

The Western Seawall

The western seawall consisted of a reef on a roughly south-north axis that may have acted as a foundation for a wall that had apparently disappeared over the years. After careful study of the western wall it is now certain that, it consists only partly of natural rock. The builders of the port apparently made clever use of the natural reef, constructing the northern and southern walls roughly on an east-west axis, connecting the reef and the shore at both the north-western and southwestern corners of the port. Round structures presumed to be watchtowers were built at the corners where the southern and the northern walls meet the natural reef.[103]

---

[103] The direction of the northern structure (breakwater?) from the shore seaward is 317°, and that of the southern structure is 259°.

Remains of the northern watchtower could still be seen at the beginning of the last century (Figure 52), and its base is still visible.

As for the western wall of the port, the natural reef, there is now ample proof that an attempt had been made to enhance its quality as a wall: On the reef itself is a narrow, shallow trench (Figure 72), very probably manmade, which seems to have served as the foundation for a structure.

Part of the structure erected on the reef, which constitutes the western wall of the port, still exists (Figure 73).

It is difficult to explain why these breakwaters (?) would have been built in regular masonry style, with the ashlars laid lengthwise, parallel to the reef, in a manner making them most vulnerable to attack by waves, and in an area most exposed to breakers. It is especially strange, since it is clear that the builders of the port were familiar with the header construction method – presenting the narrow face of the stone to the sea – as seen in the placement of the *kurkar* ashlars in the northern and southern structures which are built from *kurkar* ashlars, many of which were laid as headers.

Findings

Figure 72. The shallow trench on the reef (Photo: I. Roll)

We took samples of the joints between some stones on the reef to be chemically and petrographically tested for cement residues. If such residues are found and analysis reveals that the cement used was hydraulic, this might shed some light on the intention of the builders, which, meanwhile remains unclear in this respect.

Some pottery fragments, including the spout of a Gaza-type jar of the sixth and seventh centuries CE and other ceramic fragments, were found (mostly medieval). These were archaeologically insignificant. A modern piece of jewellery and a modern Israeli coin were found about 1.5 m under the sandy seabed, slightly to the east of the northwestern corner of the installation, which proves that sand silting at the site was ongoing over the years.

Depths

It was generally thought that the site was too shallow to have been anything but a basin that could be used only in a calm sea, which is quite rare along the open coast of the eastern Mediterranean. The probes and the excavated trench proved this to be wrong: the average depth of the sand – except where the probe hit rocks or sunken building stones, was 1.75 m, and often more, and at maximum depth some of the trenches reached hard rock at 1.0– 2.6 m below sea level. The average depth of the water was approximately 90 cm.[104]

---

[104] The water depth measurements were carried out at low tide. However, in this part of the world, the difference between high and low tide rarely exceeds 40 cm, and only during Proxigean Spring Tide, which occurs once every one and a half years. The difference between high and low tide during the research period was approximately 40 cm. The tide table for local waters at the relevant period is shown in Appendix G.

Figure 73. Remnants of structure on the reef (Photo: D. Mirkin)

If indeed the water was as deep as the probe went in and the trench excavated, then theoretically small to medium-sized vessels could have been moored in the port.

However, if the depth of the sand is disregarded and only the depth of the water measured,[105] then the port was rather shallow, especially since the sea level during the Crusader period was approximately 45 cm lower than at present according to the latest findings (Toker et al., 2012). If, on the other hand, one assumes that accumulated silt did not exist during the Crusader period, and, considering that the debris that fell from the cliff was obviously absent, then the depth of the port seems to be more reasonable, at least for small craft.

Nevertheless, the question of the shallow entrance still needs to be addressed.

Entrances

The shallow entrance by which our supplies were ferried to the excavation area in small craft most certainly would have also precluded use of the site by large vessels of any kind. However, a small boat (or, maybe, even a small galley) could be 'walked' or rowed in during an exceptionally calm

---

[105] In the Acre and Dor excavations it is customary to measure the depth of the water and disregard the depth of the sand on the seabed.

Sailing to the Holy Land

Figure 74. Supply boat walked out after dismantling the camp (Photo: A. Avidor)

sea, the depth of the water above the reef being about 60 cm at medium tide.

A geodetic surveyor was engaged to perform total station measurements in order to include all the recorded remains in the GIS site map, which resulted in Figure 75.

The GIS map (Figure 51), when enlarged, permits detailed study of the arrangement of stones and the remnants of the base of the northern tower at the north-western corner of the port (Figure 52).

Evidence of Sea Traffic near Apollonia-Arsuf

Marine traffic usually does not take place without leaving some signs, be they shipwrecks or articles, such as utensils or ceramics fallen from ships. The following table presents various items, including sherds and glassware, found underwater by Dr. Ehud Galili of the Israel Antiquities Authority. All these items were stored in the Authority's compound in Caesarea, numbered and classified.

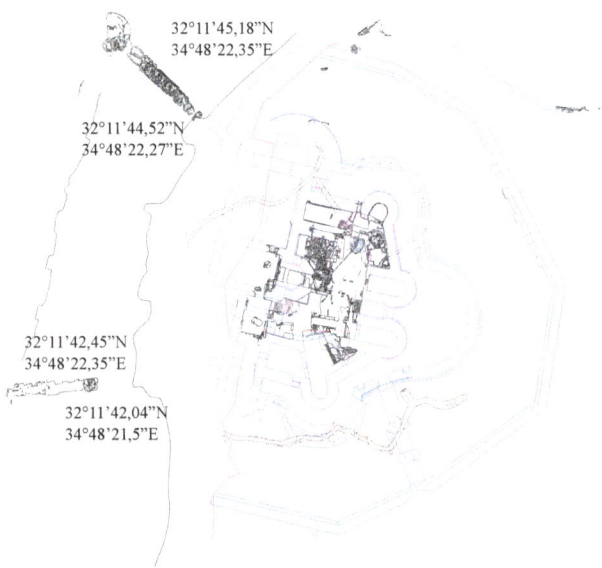

Figure 75. GIS map of the castle and outline of the installation completed 16 June 2014

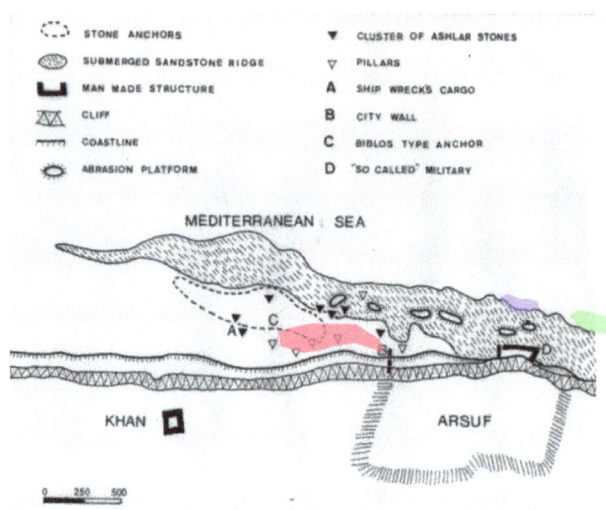

Figure 76. Locations of ceramic and glass finds near Apollonia-Arsuf

- Survey report 26/92/3
- Ceramics report 53/95/2
- Glassware Northern Area report 53/95/2

Dr. Galili's finds originating in the area of Apollonia-Arsuf are presented in the following tables. A colour-coded chart and a small map (Figure 76) show the areas where these finds were discovered.

A comparison of the above finds with those discovered in an assembly of ceramics found under water by Prof. Michal Artzy (Figure 77) in the presumed anchoring area of Crusader ships in the port of Acre (Akko), as well as with the assembly of finds in Apollonia Castle itself (Figure 78) reveals obvious similarities between the assemblages.

The similarity among all these finds, which are typical of the Crusader period, indicates robust maritime Crusader traffic in the vicinity of Apollonia-Arsuf. These include finds that

Figure 77. Underwater assembly of ceramics – Acre port, courtesy Prof. M. Artzy, (Photo M. Artzy)

Figure 78. Ceramic finds from Apollonia Castle. Courtesy Apollonia-Arsuf Excavation Project (Photos: Pavel Shrago)

Figure 79. Piece of a column found under water near Apollonia-Arsuf (Photo: O. Diamant)

Figure 80. Thin section prepared by Prof. Lorenzo Lazzarini from sample of column

reveal the foundering of vessels near Apollonia-Arsuf, or deck cargo that fell into the water.

While snorkelling about 100 m off the Apollonia-Arsuf shore in September 2010 (Lat: 32° 11' 36" N; Long: 34° 48' 15.6" E) the author and a friend found a few pieces of a column (Figure 79) approximately 40 cm in diameter. One piece was about 1.5 m long, and the other was half-buried, which made it difficult to measure. On 10 November 2010, two samples were taken, one of each column. The samples were analyzed by Professor Lorenzo Lazzarini of the Applied Petrography Department at the University IUAV of Venice. His microscopic examination of a thin slide prepared from the sample revealed that the sample (Figure 80) is Mysian granite originating in Kozak Dag, in the province of Bergama, Turkey.

This find, in conjunction with the pieces of wood and the olive pit found near the installation, tend to confirm that the area in general, and the port area in particular, were visited by ships.

It is important to note that so far it has generally been assumed that granite columns found in Apollonia were imported from Egypt. The fact that the columns found under water near the Apollonia port were made of Turkish granite may cast a different light on various thoughts concerning the origin of other columns, stones and pieces of marble from the castle of Apollonia-Arsuf.

Did Apollonia-Arsuf Have a Port?

It is tempting to call the maritime installation located at the foot of the Apollonia Arsuf castle a 'port.' Indeed, the explanatory sign directing visitors to the castle refers to the installation as a port without casting the slightest doubt, in fact, calling it 'the Crusader Port.' In her Ph.D. thesis (Grossmann 1995), Dr. Eva Grossmann included an artist's rendering showing sailing vessels moored in the so-called port. With respect, this seems to venture too far afield.

Still, whether the installation was built as a port, harbour or extension of the castle, its builders were familiar with marine building techniques. The small and difficult entrance notwithstanding, once a boat had managed to find its way into the area protected by the walls, it was relatively safe. The results of the above project show that shallow craft could be

Sailing to the Holy Land

'walked' into the port, albeit with difficulty, and that it may have been deeper about ten centuries ago, and most probably free of the debris that clutters it today. However, it could not have been a real port, although the PEF surveyors did not hesitate to label it 'HARBOUR' (see Figure 53 above and an enlarged section below, Figure 81).

In conclusion, debate over whether the installation at Apollonia-Arsuf actually served as a mooring basin, or not, has yet to be resolved, and there are valid points to be made in both directions. However, most probably it could hardly qualify as a real port.

Further underwater research in areas indicated by the sub-bottom sonar scan, especially where we found the metal impregnated piece of wood dated 1280-1400, may reveal further evidence of sea traffic in the area.

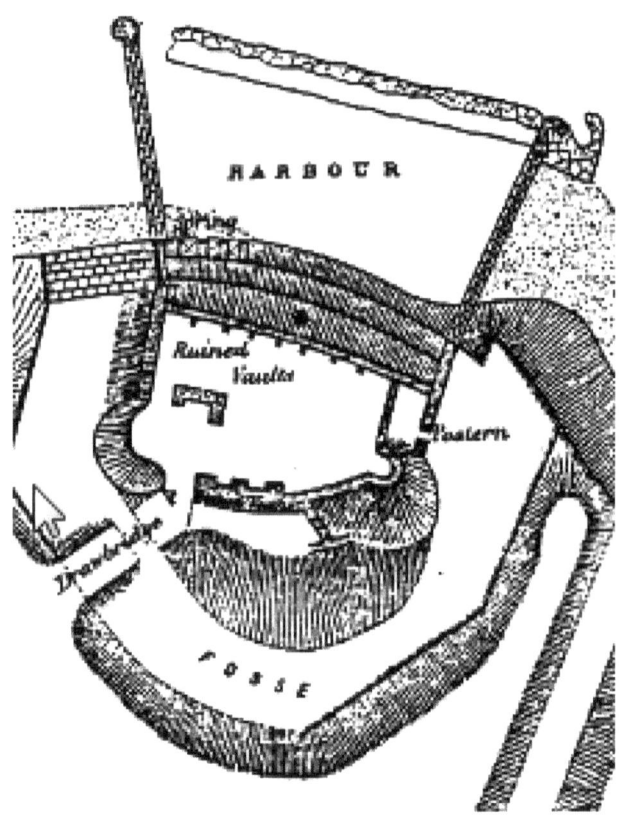

Figure 81. Section of PEF survey, Sheet 10, with the word 'HARBOUR' marked

Findings

Table 3: Underwater finds at Apollonia-Arsuf

Period	Where found	Number of item in diving report	Diving report No.	License No.	Photograph	Description
Crusader	Apollonia (green)	20	2	53/95		Two parts of a jug neck
Crusader	Apollonia (green)	16				Jug
Crusader	Apollonia (green)	17	2	53/95		Jug
Crusader 13th century	Apollonia sea			Apollonia Galili Survey 2001 19/9		Fragment of casserole
Roman-Byzantine	Apollonia sea			Apollonia Galili Survey 2001 19/9		Amphora toe
Gaza, 4th–5th century	Apollonia (red)	4	3	26/92		Jar
	Apollonia (red)	3	3	26-92		Casserole
Crusader	Apollonia (blue)	2	2	53/95		Bowl
Crusader	Apollonia (blue)	2	13	53/95		Bowl

Sailing to the Holy Land

Period	Where found	Number of item in diving report	Diving report No.	License No.	Photograph	Description
Crusader	Apollonia (blue)	2	6	53.95		Bowl
12th–13th century	Apollonia (blue)	2	1	53/95		Bowl Bi-chrome glazed
Crusader Mamluk	Apollonia (blue)	2	16	53/95		Lamp
St. Simeon 12th century	Apollonia (blue)	2	11	53/95		Bowl
St. Simeon 12th century	Apollonia (blue)	2	11	53/95		Bowl
St. Simeon 12th century	Apollonia (blue)	2	14	53/95		Bowl
Syrian import 11th–12th centuries	Apollonia (blue)	2	15	53/95		Sgraffito bowl
Late Muslim	Apollonia (blue)	2	10	53/95		Lamp
	Apollonia (blue)	2	4	53/95		Tile
Proto-Maiolica	Apollonia (blue)	2	3	53/95		Krater

Findings

Period	Where found	Number of item in diving report	Diving report No.	License No.	Photograph	Description
	Apollonia (blue)	2	12	53/95		Bowl
Late Roman	Apollonia (blue)	2	5	53/95		Lamp
Late Roman-Byzantine	Apollonia (blue)	2	7	53/95		Mould-made lamp
Late Roman-Byzantine	Apollonia (blue)	2	8	53/95		Mould-made lamp
Late Roman-Byzantine	Apollonia (blue)	2	9	53/95		Mould-made lamp

Final Thoughts

It is difficult to recapture history but visuals can assist:

The present book contains 81 Figures, a substantial part of which are iconographic images, either illuminations drawn from ancient manuscripts, church mosaics or photographs of ancient sites. The Merriam Webster dictionary defines Iconography as 'Pictorial material relating to or illustrating a subject'. Iconography is not meant to compete with archaeology, but the study of images allowed me to illustrate certain ideas, propose new thoughts, and maybe even novel solutions, to some of the questions raised in the present work. But the Iconographic analysis could not be isolated from other sources: I tried to combine it with information derived from primary and secondary written sources, and draw on my familiarity with the shores of the Levant, as well as my practical sailing experience of many years. Thus, for example, having encountered the difficulty of maneuvering the lateen sail in a blow, helped me to understand the peculiar use of the triangular sails appearing in so many images. Practical knowledge helped in solving enigmatic images, and advancing a new theory. Having beached whale boats or rowed them out through the surf along the coast of Israel, helped me to imagine the problems that the crusaders may have encountered while beaching their ships along the shores of the Holy land, which lack coves and bays. Accordingly I advanced the following theory: because the Holy Land actually had only one port – Acre, and a Jetty in Atlit, the crusaders had to prefer ships with stern opening better adapted to discharging soldiers and horses on a beach, to vessels with an opening in the side. I propose that the crusaders often chose to beach their ships rather than moor them in a port. Iconography and written sources also helped me to understand the role of small boats without which no communication could be established between ships and shore. Larger rowed boats or galleys could act as tug boats, essential in towing sail-propelled vessels and helping them to maneuvre.

It is thus the combination of Iconography, written sources, field work and practical experience which resulted in new thoughts relating to use of sails, use of ships, and use of small boats by the crusaders arriving at the shores of the Levant.

Glossary

Anchoring	Preventing the vessel from drifting by dropping an anchor from the ship to the seabed. (Mediterranean style) Anchoring the ship stern to or stem to the quay, dropping an anchor from the other end of the vessel.
Apparent wind	Wind as felt on the vessel – a combination of the true wind and the wind created by the speed of the vessel.
Athwartship	Which stretches from one side of the ship to the other. Across the ship.
Beam	The breadth measured at the widest part of the vessel.
Beam wind	Wind blowing from the side.
Bow	The foremost end of a ship, the opposite of stern.
Bowse (to)	To haul with a tackle.
Capstan	A cylindrical barrel fitted vertically near the bow of the ship, turned by means of levers or bars, used to lift heavy weights, such as hoisting anchors, or hauling on lines.
Fish (to)	To strengthen a yard or a mast on a sailing vessel by using a long piece of wood secured to the mast or yard. To tie two overlapping spars to make a longer yard, customary in lateen rigs.
Keel	The backbone of a ship. It runs along the lowest part of the hull from stem to stern.
Lateen sail	Also known as 'Lateener', a triangular sail, set on a very long yard, of which the forward end is browsed or tied well down near the bow of the vessel, set in a fore-and-aft direction, as opposed to a square sail that is set athwartship.
Lee	Away from the wind.
Leeway	Sidewise movement of the ship due to the pressure of the wind on the sail when trying to sail against the wind, and, to some extent also due to the action of the waves.
Port (side)	The left side of a vessel facing forward.
Quarter	Either side of the ship near the stern.
Quartering wind	A wind blowing from behind the vessel.
Rake	The inclination of the mast from the perpendicular. A lateen-rigged mast is raked forward; a square-rigged mast is raked back.
Reefing	Reducing the size of the sail exposed to the wind by various means.
Shrouds	Supporting lines running from the masthead to the sides of the hull. Standing rigging of a sailing vessel, which gives a mast its lateral support.
Spar	A long wooden beam, used for supporting the sails.
Square Sail	A rectangular sail set athwartship.
Starboard	The right-hand side of a vessel facing forward.
Stays	Supporting lines running from the mast to the stem or stern. Stays give the mast its fore-and-aft support.
Stem	The foremost timber of the ship, rising up from the forward end of the keel.
Stern	The rear end of the hull.
Strake	A line of planking extending the length of the vessel.
Tack	To sail at an angle to the wind closer than 90 degrees, alternating port and starboard.
True wind	The wind that actually blows (as opposed to the apparent wind).
Yard	A large spar crossing the mast of a sailing vessel horizontally or diagonally, from which a sail is set. The yard in a lateen sail consists usually of two or even three pieces.

Bibliography

Works Cited – Primary Sources

Aguilo Maria, Edició digital del Llibre dels fets del rei en Jaume I (*Libre dels feits o crònica de Jaume I*), basada en l'edició de Marià Aguiló de 1873. https://archive.org/details/Llibredelsfets (retrieved November 9, 2014).

Albert d'Aix-la-Chapelle, F. Guizot (ed.). *Histoire des faits et gestes dans les régions d'outre-mer, depuis l'année 1095 jusqu'à l'année 1120 de Jésus-Christ;* Paris: 1824.

Albert of Aix. *Historia Hierosolymitanae Expeditionis, Liber IX*, from: http://www.thelatinlibrary.com/albertofaix/hist9.shtml (retrieved December 16, 2014).

Ambroise. *L'Estoire De La Guerre Sainte, Histoire En Vers De La Troisième Croisade (1190–1192).* Gaston Paris, Editor. Paris: 1847. (web) http://gallica.bnf.fr-ark-12148-bpt6k6517331f–f265.url (Retrieved June, 2014).

Anonymous. *Histoire Anonyme de la Première Croisade.* Paris: 2002.

Belgrano, L.T. (ed.). *Annali Genovesi di Caffaro e de' Soui Continuatori Dal MXCIX al MCCXCIII*, Genova: 1890.

Boulting, W. *Four Pilgrims Hiuen–Tsiang; Saewulf; Ibn Batuta; Ludovica Varthema*, New-Delhi: 2001.

Caffaro di Rustico. Annali Genovesi di Caffaro e de'suoi continuatori *(Fonti per la storia d'Italia, Rome 1890* (trans. G. Loud). L.T. Belgrano (ed.). Rome: 1890, 79–89.

Caffaro di Rustico. *The Genoese Capture of Almeria (1147)* (trans. from Latin by G.A. Loud). In K.L. Jansen, J. Drell, F. Andrews (eds.). *Medieval Italy: Texts in Translation*. Philadelphia: 2009.

Chanson D'Antioche, Richard Le Pelerin (trans. La Marquise de Saint–Alaire). Paris: 1862. https://archive.org/stream/lachansondantio00douagoog#page/n248/mode/1up (retrieved 12 September 2014).

Clari, Robert of. *The Conquest of Constantinople* (trans. E. H. McNeal). New York: 1966.

Guillaume de Tyr, *Histoire des Croisades (bilingue),* M. Guizot (ed.). *Collection des mémoires relatif à l'histoire de France, Depuis la fondation de la monarchie française jusqu'au 13e siècle.* Paris: 1824. http:/remacle.org/bloodwolf/historiens/guillaumedetyr/table.htm (retrieved November 3, 2014).

Guizot, M. *Collection des mémoires relatif à l'histoire de France, Depuis la fondation de la monarchie française jusqu'au 13e siècle.* Paris: 1824.

Itineratum Peregrinorum Et Gesta Regis Ricardi, Stubbs, W. (ed). London: 1864.

Joinville, J. de. *Memoires du Sir de Joinville ou histoire de Saint Louis*, Paris: 1867.

Joinville, J. de. *Vie de Saint Louis.* Paris: 1995.

Saewulf 1892. *The Pilgrimage of Saewulf to Jerusalem and the Holy Land in the Years 1102 and 1103* (trans. M.A. Brownlaw). London: 1892.

Sanudo, Marino Torsello. *The Book of the Secrets of the Faithful of the Cross, Liber Secretorum Fidelium Crucis* (trans. P. Lock). Farnham: 2011.

Sweetenham, C. *Robert Monk's History of the First Crusade, Historia Hierosolimitana.* Oxford: 2005.

Tsamakda, V. *The Illustrated Chronicle of Ioannes Skylitzes in Madrid.* Leiden, 2002.

Villehardouin, G. and Joinville, J. de. *Joinville and Villehardouin Chronicles of the Crusades* (trans. with an introduction and notes by C. Smyth). London: 2008.

Ville-Hardouin, G. de. *Histoire de la Conquête de Constaninople, avec la continuation de Henri de Valencinnes* (transformed into modern French by M. Natalis de Wailly). Paris: 1870.

Vitry: Lettres de Jacques de Vitry, R.B.C. Huygens (ed.). No. 2 (trans. I. Rau). Leiden: 1960, 79–97. http://www.leeds.ac.uk/arts/.../a_letter_of_jacques_de_vitry_121617.

William of Tyre. *History of Deeds Done Beyond the Sea,* Medieval Sourcebook, Chapter 6 (XVII, 22–25, 27–30). http://www.fordham.edu/halsall/source/tyre–cde.html (retrieved October 23, 2014).

William of Tyre. *History of Deeds Done Beyond the Sea,* Volumes I and II. New York: 1976.

Works Cited – Secondary Sources

Artzy, M. Looking for a Phoenician Harbour. (*R.I.M.S News*, University of Haifa, Leon Recanati Institute for Maritime Studies Report 38). 2012–2013, 12–14.

Asbridge, T. *The Crusades,* London, 2012.

Baha' al-Din. *What Befell Sultan Yusuf* (trans. C.W. Wilson). London: 1897.

Balard, M. and Picard, C. *La Méditerranée au Moyen Âge*, Paris: 2014.

Bass, G.F. *A History of Seafaring Based on Underwater Archaeology.* New York: 1972.

Bonino, M. Lateen-rigged medieval ships. New evidence from wrecks in the Po Delta (Italy) and notes on pictorial and other documents, *The International Journal of Nautical and Underwater Exploration,* 1978, 7.1, 9-28.

Broadhurst, R.J.C. *The Travels of Ibn Jubayr.* London: 1951.

Brown, A.L. *The Story of Maps,* Boston: 1949.

Buchon, J.A. *Recherches Historiques sur la Principauté Française de Morée et ses Hautes Baronnes. Le Livre de la Conqueste, Première Période, Tome Premier,* Paris: 1845.

Burningham, N. and de Jong, A. The Duyfken Project: an Age of Discovery ship reconstruction as experimental archaeology. *International Journal of Nautical Archaeology.* 1997, 26.4, 277–292. http://onlinelibrary.wiley.com/doi/10.1111/j.1095–9270.1997.tb01339.x/pdf (retrieved October 15, 2014).

Campbell, I.C. The Lateen Sail in World History. *Journal of World History* 6:1 1995. http://www.uhpress.hawaii.edu/journals/jwh/jwh061p001.pdf (retrieved April 5, 2015).

Casson, L. Speed Under Sail of Ancient Ships. *Transactions of the American Philological Association* 82, 1951, 136–148. http://penelope.uchicago.edu/Thayer/E/Journals/TAPA/82/Speed_under_Sail_of_Ancient_Ships*.html (retrieved August 16, 2014).

Casson, L. *Ships and Seamanship in the Ancient World*. Baltimore: 1995.

Conder, C.R. and Kitchener, H.H. 1882. *The Survey of Western Palestine* II: *Samaria*. London: 1882, 137–140.

Cvikel, D., Kahanov, Y. and Artzy, M. Akko Underwater Excavation – Report of the 2012 Season. *R.I.M.S. News,* University of Haifa, Leon Recanati Institute for Maritime Studies 38, 2013, 10–14

De Sandoli, S. *Itinera Hieroslymitana Crucesignatorum* (saec. XII–XIII). II. Jerusalem: 1978.

Dotson, J.E. Fleet Operations in the First Genoese–Venetian War, 1264–1266. *Viator* 30, 1999, 165–180.

Dotson, J.E. Ship Types and Fleet Composition. In *Logistics of Warfare in the Age of the Crusades*. J.H. Pryor (ed.). Aldershot: 2006, 63–75.

Eisenstein, J.D. *The Compendium of Jewish Travels*. New York: 1926 (Hebrew).

Erlich, M. The Battle of Arsur: A Short–Lived Victory. *Journal of Medieval Military History* 12, 2014, 110–118.

Explore Archives and Manuscripts – British Library: http://prodigi.bl.uk/IllImages/Kslides%5Cmid/K038/K038466.jpg (retrieved October 2014.

Fabri, F. *The Book of the Wanderings of Brother Felxi Fabri* (trans. A. Stewart). London: 1896.

Flatman, J.C. 'The iconographic evidence for maritime activities in the Middle Ages. *Current Science* 86:9, 2004, 1276–1282.

Flatman, J. *The Illuminated Ark: Interrogating Evidence from Manuscript Illuminations and Archaeological Remains for Medieval Vessels*. (BAR International Series 1616). Oxford: 2007.

Flatman, J. *Ships and Shipping in Medieval Manuscripts.* London: 2009.

Flemming, N.C., Raban, A. and Goetschel, C. Tectonic and Eustatic Changes on the Mediterranean Coast of Israel in the Last 9000 Years. *Progress in Underwater Science* 3, 1978, 33–93.

Folda, J. *Crusader Manuscript Illumination at Saint–Jean d'Acre 1275–1291.* Princeton: 1976.

Folda, J. *Crusader Art: the Art of the Crusaders in the Holy Land.* Aldershot: 2008.

Galili, E., and Sharvit, Y. Findings of underwater survey in Yavneh-Yam. In *Yavneh, Yavneh-Yam and their Neighborhood. Studies in the Archaeology and History of the Judean Coastal Plain.* M. Fischer (ed.). Tel Aviv: 2005, 303–314.

Galili, E. Rosen, B., Zviely, D., Silberstein, N. and Finkelsztjen, G. The Evolution of Akko Harbour and its Mediterranean Maritime Trade Links *Journal of Island and Coastal Archaeology,* 5, 2010, 191–211.

Gillingham, J. *Richard I.* New Haven and London: 1999.

Gluzman, R. Between Venice and the Levant: Re-evaluating Maritime Routes From the Fourteenth to the Sixteenth Century, *The Mariner's Mirror,*2010, 96:3, 264-294

Grossmann, E. *Maritime Investigation of Tel-Michal and Apollonia Sites.* (Ph.D. diss., Macquerie University) North Ryde, Australia: 1995.

Grossmann, E. and Kingsley, S.A. A Three-hole Stone Anchor with Wood Remains from Crusader Arsuf (Apollonia). *International Journal of Nautical Archaeology* 25, 1996, 49–54.

Grossmann, E. Maritime Apollonia (Arsuf) and Its Harbours. *Mariner's Mirror* 83, 1997, 80–84. .

Grossmann, E. *Maritime Tel Michal and Apollonia: Results of the Underwater Survey 1989–1996* (BAR International Series 915). Oxford: 2001. .

Grousset, R. *Histoire des croisades I 1095–1130, l'Anarchie Musulman,* Paris: 1934 (repr. 2006).

Grousset, R. *Histoire des croisades II 1131–1187, l'équilibre,* Paris: 1934 (repr. 2006).

Grousset, R. *L'épopée des croisades.* Paris: 2002.

Haggi, A. Report on Underwater Excavation at the Phoenician Harbour, Atlit, Israel *The International Journal of Nautical Archaeology* 39.2, 2010, 278–285.

Jabour, E., *Sailing and seamanship in the 12th Century in the Mediterranean, Nile and the Red Sea, based on the travels of Ibn Jubayr.* Thesis submitted in partial fulfilment of the requirements for the Master's Degree, University of Haifa. Haifa: 2012. (Hebrew).

Jacoby, D. The Supply of War Materials to Egypt in the Crusader Period. *Jerusalem Studies in Arabic and Islam,* 25, 2001, 102–134. Repr. in Jacoby, D. *Commercial Exchange across the Mediterranean: Byzantium, the Crusader Levant, Egypt and Italy*. Aldershot: 2005, 102–132.

Jacoby, D. A Venetian Sailing to Acre in 1282: Between Private Shipping and Privately Operated State Galleys. In Laudem Hierosolymitani: *Studies in Crusades and Medieval Culture in Honour of Benjamin Z. Kedar.* I. Shagrir, R. Ellenblum and J. Riley-Smith (eds.). Aldershot: 2007a, 395–410.

Jacoby, D. Hospitaller Ships and Transportation across the Mediterranean. In *The Hospitallers, the Mediterranean and Europe. Festschrift for Anthony Luttrell.* K. Borchardt, N. Jaspert and H.J. Nicholson (eds.). Aldershot: 2007b, 57–72.

Jacoby, D. Amalfi nell'xi secolo: commercio e navigazione nei documenti della Ghenizà del Cairo. In *Rassegna del Centro di cultura e storia amalfitana, 36,* Amalfi :2008, 81-90

Jacoby, D. An Unpublished Medieval Portolan of the Mediterranean in Minneapolis. In *Shipping, Trade and Crusade in the Medieval Mediterranean, Studies in Honour of John Pryor*. R. Gertwagen and E. Jeffreys (eds.). Farnham: 2012, 65–83.

Jal, A. *Archéologie Navale*. Paris: 1840.

Kahanov, Y. and Jabour, I., The Westbound Passage of Ibn Jubayr from Acre to Cartagena,1184-1185. In *Al-Masāq: Islam and the Medieval Mediterranean*, 22.1, 2010, 79–101.

Kahanov, Y., The Dor/Tantura Shipwrecks: Clues to their Construction Tradition in *Archaeologia Maritima Mediterranea, 8,* 2011, 137-151.

Kedar, B.Z. The Outer Walls of Frankish Acre, *Atiquot 31,* 1997 157-180.

Kedar, B.Z. King Richard's Plan for the Battle of Arsuf/Arsur, 1191. In *The Medieval Way of War: Studies in Medieval Military History in Honor of Bernard S. Bachrach.* G.I. Halfond (ed.). Aldershot: 2015, 117–132.

Kemp, P. (ed.) *The Oxford Companion to Ships and the Sea,* Oxford: 2005.

Landström, B. *Sailing Ships.* London: 1969.

Long, P.O. McGee D. and Stahl A,M. *The Book of Michael of Rhodes, a Fifteenth-Century Maritime Manuscript,* Vol. 3. (rev/expanded). Cambridge, Massachusetts: 2009.

Madden, T.F. *The New Concise History of the Crusades.* Oxford: 2006

Mantzourani, E. and Theodorou, A. An attempt to delineate the sea routes between Crete and Cyprus during the Bronze Age. In *The Civilizations of the Aegean and their Diffusion in Cyprus and the Eastern Mediterranean, 2000–600 BC: Proceedings of an International Symposium 18–24 September 1989.* V. Karageorghis (ed.). Larnaca: 1989, 38–56.

Martin, L.R. *The Art and Archaeology of Venetian Ships and Boats.* College Station: 2001.Martin, L.R. Horse and cargo handling on Medieval Mediterranean ships. *The International Journal of Nautical Archaeology* 31.2, 2002, 237–247.

Mayer, H.E. *The Crusades.* Oxford: 1991.

McGrail, S. Navigational techniques in Homer's Odyssey. In *Tropis IV: 4th international symposium on ship construction in Antiquity, Athens 1991.* H. Tzalas (ed.). Athens: 1996, 311–320.

McGrail, S. *Boats of the World from the Stone Age to Medieval Times.* Oxford: 2001.

Mirkin, D. *A Port without a Port: The Port of Jaffa during the Ottoman Period (1516–1917) According to Travellers' Descriptions, Photographs and Iconography,* Thesis submitted in partial fulfillment of the requirements for the Master's Degree, University of Haifa. Haifa: 2010 (Hebrew).

Mirkin, D. The Ottoman Port of Jaffa: A Port without a Harbour. In *The History and Archaeology of Jaffa 2*, Aaron A. Burke, Katherine Strange Burke and Martin Peilstocker, Editors; Monumenta Archaeologica 41, Cotsen Institute of Archaeology Press, University of California, Los Angeles: 2017, 121-155.

Mirkin, D. and Goren, H. Jaffa– a Port without a Port: Failure of the Ninteenth–century Plans to build a Modern Deep–water Port. *Cathedra* 143, 2012, 133–152 (Hebrew).

Mollat, M. Problèmes maritimes de l'histoire des croisades. In *Cahiers de civilizations médiévales.* 10e année (No 39–40), Juillet–Décembre 1967, 345–359.

Morozzo Della Rocca, R. and Lombardo A. *Documenti del Commercio Veneziano Nei Secoli XI–XIII* (Two Volumes). Torino: 1940.

Muraro, M. *Paolo da Venezia,* University park: Pennsylvania State University Press: 1970.

Murray, W.M. Do Modern Winds Equal Ancient Winds? *Mediterranean Historical Review* 2, 1987, 139–167.

Nicholson, H.J. *Chronicle of the Third Crusade, a Translation of the* Itinerarum Peregrinorum et Gesta Regis Ricardi. Aldershot and Vermont: 1997.

Nicholson, H. *Love, War and the Grail.* Leiden: 2001.

Nicholson, H. (ed.). *The Crusaders.* Chippenham: 2005.

Norie, J.W. *New Piloting Directions for the Mediterranean Sea.* London: 1831.

Palmer, C. Windward Sailing Capabilities of Ancient Vessels. *The International Journal of Nautical Archaeology* 38.2, 2009, 314–330.

Pomey, P. The Kelenderis Ship: A Lateen Sail. *The International Journal of Nautical Archaeology* 35.2, 2006, 326–335.

Prawer, J. *The Crusaders, a Colonial Society.* Jerusalem: 1985 (Hebrew).

Pryor, J.H. Transportation of Horses by Sea during the Era of the Crusaders: Eighth Century to 1285 A.D. *Mariner's Mirror* 68.1, 1982a, 9–27; 68.2: 103–126.

Pryor, J.H. Reply to Fourquin's note, Notes about the transportation of horses by sea during the era of the Crusades, part II by John Pryor. *Mariner's Mirror,* 68: 1982b, 389–390.

Pryor, J.H. 'The Naval Architecture of Crusader Transport Ships. A Reconstruction of Some Archetypes for Round-Hulled Sailing Ships.' *Mariner's Mirror* 70, 1984, 171–219; Part II, 271–292; Part III, 363–386.

Pryor, J.H. and Jeffreys, E.M. *The Age of the ΔPOMON: The Byzantine Navy ca 500–1204*, Boston: 2006.

Pryor, J.H. A Medieval Mediterranean Maritime Revolution: Crusading by Sea ca. 1096-1204, in *Maritime Studies in the Wake of the Byzantine Shipwreck at Yassiada, Turkey,* Deborah N. Carlson, Editor; Texas: 2015, 174-188.

Raban, A. Caesarea-Yam, In *The New Encyclopedia of Archaeological Excavations in the Holy Land* 4, E. Stern (ed.). Jerusalem: 1992, 1385–1391 (Hebrew).

Raban, A. and Linder, E. Atlit–Yam. In *The New Encyclopedia of Archaeological Excavations in the Holy Land* 4, E. Stern (ed.). Jerusalem: 1992, 1289–1292 (Hebrew).

Recueil des Historiens des Croisades. Historiens Occidentaux. Paris: 1854.

Richard of the Holy Trinity, Itinerary of Richard I and others to the Holy Land (trans. 'A classical scholar'). Cambridge: 2001. http://www.yorku.ca/inpar/richard_of_holy_trinity.pdf (retrieved November 30, 2014).

Rubenstein, J. *Armies of Heaven, the First Crusade and the Quest for Apocalypse,* New York: 2011.

Shipley, D. and Graham, J. Pseudo–Skylax and the Natural Philosophers. *Journal of Hellenic Studies* 132, 2012, 121–138.

Sivéry, G. *Philippe Auguste.* Paris: 1993.

Smith, D. and Buffery, H. *The Book of Deeds of James of Aragon, A Translation of the Medieval Catalan Libre del Fets.* Aldershot: 2003.

Smyth, W.H. *The Mediterranean: A Memoir – Physical, Historical and Nautical.* London: 1854.

Sterling, D. The Siege of Damietta, Sea Power in the Fifth Crusade. In *Medieval Warfare in Societies around the Mediterranean.* D.J. Kagay and A.L.J. Villalon (eds). Leiden–Boston: 2003, 101– 131.

Tal, O., Charpak, T., Ziffer, I. and Haggi, Y. *The Last Supper in Apollonia,* Tel Aviv: 2011.

Toker, E., Sivan, D., Stern, E., Shirman, B. Tsimplis, M., Spada, G. 2012. Evidence for centennial scale sea level variability during the Medieval Climate Optimum (Crusader Period) in Israel, eastern Mediterranean. *Earth and Planetary Science Letters*. 315-316, 51-61.

Tsamakada, V. *The Illustrated Chronicle of Ioannes Skylitzes in Madrid,* Ledien: 2002.

United States Hydrographic Office. *Sailing directions for the Mediterranean: volume IV, Libya, Egypt, Turkey (Southern Coast), Syria, Lebanon Palestine, and the Islands of Crete Scarpanto, Rhodes, and Cyprus*. Washington: 1951.

Wachsmann, S. and Raveh, K. A Concise Nautical History of Dor/Tantura; *International Journal of Nautical Archaeology* 13, 1984, 223–241.

Whitewright, J. The Potential Performance of Ancient Mediterranean Sailing Rigs, *International Journal of Nautical Archaeology* 40.1, 2011[a], 2–17.

Whitewright, J. Efficiency or Economics? Sail development in the Ancient Mediterranean (*JRA* Supplementary Series 84). Portsmouth, R.I., 2011[b], 89–103. https://www.academia.edu/936867/Efficiency_or_Economics_Sail_development_in_the_ancient_Mediterranean.

Wilson, C. *Picturesque Palestine,* III. London: 1881.

Wolff, R.L. and Hazard, H.W. (eds.). The Later Crusades, 1189–1311. In *A History of the Crusades,* II. Madison and Milwaukee, Wisc.–London: 1969. http://digital.library.wisc.edu/1711.dl/History.CrusTwo.

Yaari, A. *Jewish Travels to the Land of Israel from the Middle Age until the Beginning of the Return to Zion.* Ramat Gan: 1977 (Hebrew).

General Bibliography

Aquensis Albericus (Albert d'Aix), *Histoire des faits et gestes dans les régions d'outre-mer, depuis l'année 1096, jusqu'au l'année1120 de Jésus Christ,* Livre IX (*Historia Hieroslymitanae Expeditionis, Liber Nonus).*

Asbridge, T. *The First Crusade.* Oxford: 2004.

Balard, M. Les transports maritimes Genois vers la terre sainte, in: *I Comuni Italiani nel regno crociato di Gerusalemme.* G. Airaldi and B.Z. Kedar (eds.). Genoa: 1986, 143–174.

Basch, L. *Le musée imaginaire de la marine antique.* Athens: 1987.

Bass, G.F. *A History of Seafaring Based on Underwater Archaeology,* New York: 1972.Bernstein, D.J. *The Mystery of the Bayeux Tapestry.* London: 1986.

Billion, P. A Newly Discovered Chart Fragment from the Lucca Archives, Italy. *Imago Mundi: The International Journal for the History of Cartography* 63:1, 2011, 1–21.

Bradford, E. *Mediterranean: Portrait of a Sea*, London: 1971.

Bramoullé, D. Activités navales et insfrastructures maritimes :éléments du pouvoir fatimide en Méditerranée orientale (969–1171). In *Les Ports et la Navigation en Méditerranée au Moyen Age.* Lattes: 2008, 253–269.

Byrne, E. H., *Genoese Shipping in the Twelfth and Thirteenth Centuries*, Cambridge: 1930.

Cvikel, D. and Goren H. Where are Bonaparte's Siege Cannon? An Episode in the Egyptian Campaign. *Mediterranean Historical Review* 23/2, 2008, 129–142.

Dale, S., Williams Lewin A. and Osheim, D.J. (eds.). *Chronicling History: Chroniclers and Historians in Medieval and Renaissance Italy.* University Park, Pennsylvania: 2007.

De La Roncière C. and Clerc–Rampal, G., *Histoire de la marine Française*, Paris: 1934.

De Villehut, B. *Le Manoeuvrier ou Essai sur la Théorie et la Pratique des Mouvements du Navire et des Évolutions navales,* Paris: 1765.

Epstein, A.S. *Genoa and the Genoese.* North Carolina: 1996Flori, J. *Richard Coeur de Lion: Le roi chevalier.* Paris: 1999.

France, J. Crusading Warfare. In *The Crusaders.* H. Nicholson (ed.). Chippenham: 2005, 58–82.

Grossmann, E. and Kingsley, S.A. A Three-hole Stone Anchor with Wood Remains from Crusader Arsuf (Apollonia). *International Journal of Nautical Archaeology* 25, 1996, 49–54.

Grossmann, E. Maritime Apollonia (Arsuf) and Its Harbours. *Mariner's Mirror* 83, 1997, 80–84.

Grossmann, E., *Maritime Tel Michal and Apollonia: Results of the Underwater Survey 1989–1996,* Oxford: 2001.

Harley, J.B. and Woodward, D. *The History of Cartography,* I: *Cartography in Prehistoric, Ancient and Medieval Europe and the Mediterranean.* London: 1987.

Hohlfelder, R.L., Oleson, J.P., Raban, A. and Lindley Vann, R. Sebastos: Herod's Harbour at Caesarea Maritima. *Biblical Archaeologist* 46, 1983, 133–143.

Hofmann, C., Richard, H. and Vagnon, E. *l'Age d'or des Cartes Marines,* Paris: 2012.

Hopkins, F.N. *Norie's Nautical Tables with Explanations of Their Use.* Saint Ives, Huntington, U.K.: 1973.

Hourani, G.F. *Arab Seafaring in the Indian Ocean in Ancient and Early Medieval Times* Beirut: 1963.

Hutchisson, G. *Medieval Ships and Shipping.* Rutheford: 1994.

Jacoby, D. Amalfi nell' XI secolo: commercio e navigazione nei documenti della Ghenizà del Cairo. *Rassegna del Centro di Cultura e Storia Amalfitana* 36, 2008, pp. 81–90.

Jankrift, K.P. International Mobility in the Order of St. Lazarus (Twelfth to Early Fourteenth Centuries). In *International Mobility in the Military Orders (Twelfth to Fifteenth Centuries): Travelling on Christ's Business.* J. Burgstorf and H. Nicholson (eds.).Cardiff: 2006, 59–64.

Jonquière, Clément, de la. *L'expédition d'Egypte 1798–1801,* IV Paris: 1899–1907.

Kahanov, Y., Cvikel, D., Wielinski, A. and Israeli E. Dor Underwater Excavation – Report of the 2008 Season. *R.I.M.S. News, University of Haifa Leon Recanati Institute for Maritime Studies* 34, 2008, 15–19.

Kahanov, Y. Ancient Shipwrecks in Dor/Tantura Lagoon and their Significance. *Cathedra* 134, 2009, 5–24 (Hebrew, English abstract).

Kahanov, Y. Ship Reconstruction, Documentation, and In Situ Recording. In *The Oxford Handbook of Maritime Archaeology.* A. Catambis, B. Ford, and D. Hamilton (eds.). Oxford: 2011, 161–181.

Lambert, C.L. *Shipping the Medieval Military, English Maritime Logistics in the Fourteenth Century.* Woodbridge: 2011.

Lane, F.C. *Venetian Ships and Shipbuilding of the Renaissance.* New York: 1979.

Levy-Rubin, M. Crusader Maps of Jerusalem. In *Holy Land in Maps.* A. Tishby (ed.). Jerusalem: 2001, 136–139,

Maaluf, A. *The Crusades Through Arab Eyes* (trans. J. Rothschild). New York: 1984.

Marks, R.F. *The Underwater Dig*, New York: 1975.

Martoni, D.N. *Il Pellegrino di Luoghi Santi da Carinola a Gerusalemme 1394–1395.* Paris: 2003.

Navri, R. Dor 2006 Shipwreck – Report of the 2009 Excavation Season. *R.I.M.S. News, University of Haifa Leon Recanati Institute for Maritime Studies* 35, 2009, 20–21.

Ökte, E.Z. (ed.). *Kitab–I Bahriye Piri Reis.* Istanbul: 1988.

Papageorgiou, D.. The marine environment and its influence on seafaring and maritime routes in the prehistoric Aegean. *European Journal of Archaeology* 11.2–3, 2009, 199–222.

Powell, J.M. *Anatomy of a Crusade 1213–1221.* Philadelphia: 1986.

Pryor, J.H. *Geography Technology, and War: Studies in the Maritime History of the Mediterranean 649–1571.* New York: 1988.

Pryor, J.H. The Naval Architecture of Crusader Transport Ships and Horse Transports Revisited. *The Mariner's Mirror* 76, 1990, 255–273.

Pryor, J.H. The Geographical Conditions of Galley Navigation in the Mediterranean. In *The Age of the Galley: Mediterranean*

Oared Vessels since Pre–Classical Times. R. Gardiner (ed.). London: 1995, 206–216.

Pryor, J.H. Water, water everywhere, Nor any drop to drink. Water supplies for the fleets of the First Crusade. In *Dei gesta per Francos, Etudes sur les croisades dédiées à Jean Richard – Crusade studies in honour of Jean Richard,* M. Balard, B.Z. Kedar and J. Riley-Smith (eds.). Aldershot: 2001.

Pryor, J.H. A View From a Masthead: The First Crusade from the Sea. *Crusades* 7, 2008, 87–151.

Pryor, J.H. Ships of the Crusade Era, Part II. http://weaponsandwarfare.com/?p=102 (retrieved Aug. 16, 2014).

Purdy, J. *The New Sailing Directions for the Mediterranean Sea, the Adriatic Sea or Gulf of Venice, the Archipelago and Levant.* London: 1826.

Richards, D.S. *The Chronicle of Ibn al-Athir for the Crusading Period from al Kāmil fi'l–ta'rikh.* Part 3: *The Years 589–629/1231: The Ayyubids after Saladin and the Mongol Menace.* Aldershot and Vermont: 2008.

Richon, L. Les nefs des Croisades. *Neptunia* 101, 1971, 1–5.

Rogers, W.L. *Naval Warfare under Oars 4th to 16th Centuries,* Annapolis: 1988.

Roll, I., Tal, O. and Winter, M. (eds.). *The Encounter of Crusaders and Muslims in Palestine,* Tel Aviv: 2007. (Hebrew).

Roncière, C. de, *Histoire de la marine française.* Paris: 1899.

Rose, S. *Medieval Naval Warfare, 1000–1500,* London and New York: 2002.

Rubin de Cervin, G.B. *La Flotta di Venezia.* Milano: 1985.

The Rules of Oleron. n.a. http://www.admiraltylawguide.com/documents/oleron.html. (retrieved July 21, 2014).

Teterycz-Puzio, A. *Henryk Sandomierski Polski Krzyzowiec,* Krakow: 2015.

Tsafrir, Y. The Madaba Map. In *Holy Land in Maps.* A. Tishby (ed.). Jerusalem: 2001, 66–71.

Unger, R.W. Warships and Cargo Ships in Medieval Europe. *Technology and Culture* 22, 1981, 233–252.

Verdon, J. *Voyager au Moyen Age.* Paris: 2007.

Watts, A. *Wind Pilot,* Hampshire: 1971.

Wells, C. *Sailing from Byzantium.* New York: 2006.

APPENDICES

Appendix A

Sonar Investigation

The Harbour of

Apollonia-Arsuf

Oct-Nov 2010

by

Hans Günter Martin[106]

---

[106] The report in Appendix A has not been edited. When this report was prepared Dr. Günter Martin, a scientist, was affiliated with DEGUWA – Deutsche Gesellschaft zur Förderung der Unterwasserarchäologie e. V.

The Harbour of Apollonia-Arsuf

Acknowledgements

Apollonia is a great and important place and we were happy to work there. During our two weeks stay we received help from all sides, for which we are thankful.

In first place we want to thank Oren Tal and Dan Mirkin for their precious help and warm hospitality.

A preliminary remark

The illustrations added to the printed version of this report allow a fast overview on the results of the sonar analyses. For better work we recommend opening the files on the joint CD where you can choose the size of the illustrations.

This report assumes that the reader is familiar with the possibilities and the limits of the methods of sonar analysing. Basically the sonar is measuring just the density of different materials. There is no information in the sonar data about the nature and the age of the objects.

A colour scale with seven numbered steps is added to the illustrations of the sonar cuts. Each step represents the signal strength that way: number of colour multiplied by 20db gives the intensity; for instance the green: 2*20db=40db or the red: 6*20db=120db and so on.

Tech Talk

The collection of the data took place from 9-30-2010 to 10-6-2010. The survey was carried out by Dr. K. Storch (SOSO-Jena), the inventor and longtime user of this special sediment-sonar and by myself (abatonos). The equipment was mounted onto a small RIB steered by the tireless Arieh (Duba) Diamant. We want to thank him explicitly for that.

The sediment sonar in use is a perpendicular bifrequential sonar. The transducer produces two signals of constant strength. The reflections are measured. It allows under most circumstances to penetrate the sediment until the bedrock and to locate all hard findings or objects lying in there. The positioning was done by a combined DGPS. All positions are given in dd.dddd° in WGS 84.

Comment

To complete the long and successful excavations in Apollonia-Arsuf the director of this excavation Prof Dr Oren Tal is planning to study also the harbour or better to say the harbours, situated immediately at the foot of the cliff (ill.40).

There is already a study of the harbours from the 90s done and presented by Eva Grossmann (Maritime Tel Michal and Apollonia. Results of the underwater survey 1989-1996. In: BAR S915, 2001). She achieved remarkable results only by diving in these very often rough waters. The time has come for an amplified study. In the first step a sonar investigation was to execute to determine places where full excavation would be promising and where there is nothing to expect.

In the period when we did the sonar investigation the weather was fine, but we had often a relatively high swell that made it a little bit difficult to go by RIB to all places in the harbour. Nevertheless we achieved good coverage except of the most northern part of the harbour. In the so-called Crusaders harbour the bottom is completely covered by stones and pebbles that prevent the sonar signal to go underneath. Therefore no significant statement could be achieved from the data collected and this part was left out.

We should think about another method of prospection in the Crusaders harbour, but for the moment I have no solution. Most of the stones lying in the basin do not belong there, but they had fallen down from the hill. The scientific dilemma of the basin: is it a harbour and under the stones there is maritime material or is it a substructure of an architectural building and under stones there are walls, is not to decide by the sonar.

There was a vague possibility that the actual western edge of the harbour is not the original one, but there could be a kind of mole more to the West. To check this we measured also outside the harbour and thus the data are divided into two sections: the out area (ill. 1 - 21) and the inside area (ill. 22 - 39).

One initial remark regarding the system of the illustrations: in the post processing of the data we did a virtual excavation with layers in -20, -40, -80, -100, and 120 cm. The "digging tool" is on one hand the low frequency and on the other hand the high frequency. The result is a bit like in land excavation: you remove the earth and you see the surface of the layer. Pictures of this kind are named "cut", LF for low frequency and HF for high frequency. In addition to that you have the picture with the surface of the layer and all signals below that. It is like in land excavation when you remove the earth around the findings leaving them in situ and you go deeper into the soil. It gives you an idea of the continuation of the findings into the depth. Pictures of this kind are named "sum up", LF for low frequency and HF for high frequency. Generally you have 4 pictures for each layer (see the following list).

Layers and Illustration-Numbers

out area		inside area	
layer	ill.-no.	layer	ill.-no.
LF -20cm cut	2	LF -20cm cut	22
LF -20cm sum up	3	LF -20cm sum up	23
HF -20cm cut	4	HF -20cm cut	24
HF -20cm sum up	5	HF -20cm sum up	25
LF -40cm cut	6	LF -40cm cut	26
LF -40cm sum up	7	LF -40cm sum up	27
HF -40cm cut	8	HF -40cm cut	28
HF -40cm sum up	9	HF -40cm sum up	29
LF -80cm cut	10	LF -80cm cut	30
LF -80cm sum up	11	LF -80cm sum up	31
HF -80cm cut	12	HF -80cm cut	32
HF -80cm sum up	13	HF -80cm sum up	33
LF -100cm cut	14	LF -100cm cut	34
LF -100 sum up	15	LF -100cm sum up	35
HF -100cm cut	16	HF -100cm cut	36
HF -100cm sum up	17	LF -120cm cut	37
LF -120 cut	18	LF -120cm sum up	38
LF -120cm sum up	19	HF -120cm cut	39
HF -120cm cut	20		
HF -120cm sum up	21		

The area west to the harbour (out area)

In the depth profile (ill. 1) you can see the "foot" of the harbour wall consisting of beach rock shown mostly in red. Towards the open sea the bottom is sloping down gradually. When you put the high frequency cuts (ill. 4, 8, 12, 16, 20) to a row, the development of the beach rock into the depth is clearly visible.

Looking at the sonar data there is a first result: the idea of another outer harbour wall in this to give up, there is no wall. We have to take the existing beach rock wall as the western limitation of the harbour.

Since we are immediately outside the harbour some shipwrecks are to be expected, because approaching a harbour or mooring outside is one of the most dangerous moments for a ship. We have a lot of evidence for that in other places. Indeed there are six places to individuate that might be suspicious to represent wreck sites. They are shown here in this text illustration as red dots.

Appendix A

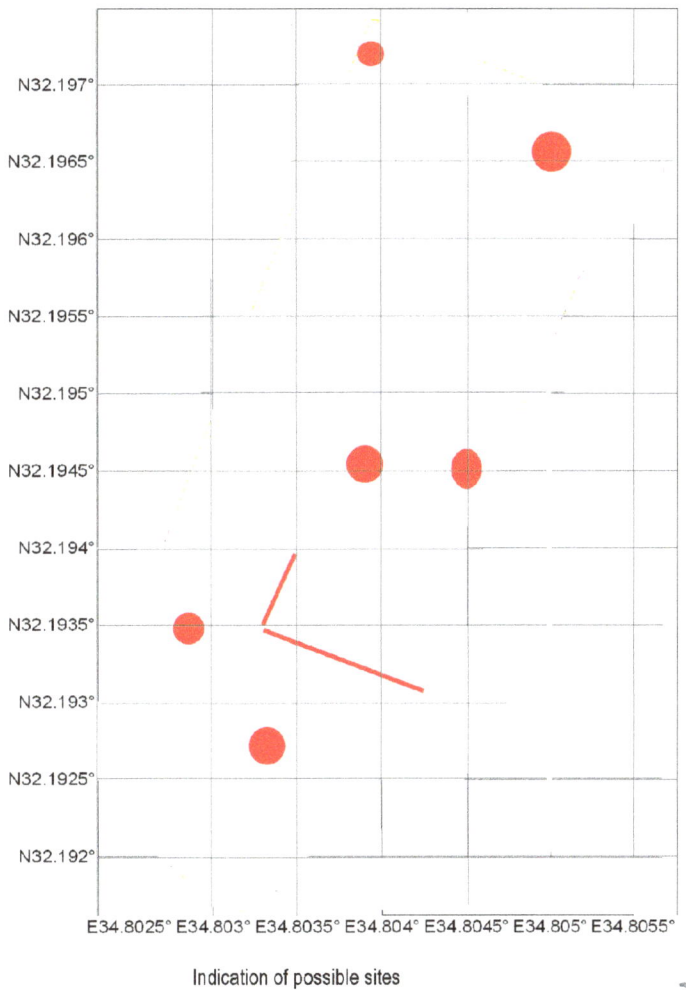

Indication of possible sites

Going from north to South the first site in the northwest corner of the measured area is best to see in the HF sum up -20 cm (ill. 12), but also in the other HF sum ups (ill. 9,13,17,21) and also in the HF cuts from -80 cm on and deeper (ill. 12,16,20). The area has the extension of about 25 m with a solid nucleus of about 10 m.

The second site is situated near the North east corner of the measured area. It shows up in the HF sum ups -80 cm and deeper (ill. 13,17,21). It is present also in the HF cuts -80 cm and deeper (ill. 12,16,20).

In the middle of the area there are two more sites, one at the eastern edge and the other about 60 m west to it. You can see them in the HF cut -80 cm (ill. 12) and also in the LF cut -100 cm (ill. 14). In the LF sum up -40 cm they are represented in magenta.

Another site is situated in the prolongation of the actual western entrance of the harbour. It is shown in orange in the HF cut -100 cm (ill. 16) and also in the HF sum up - 20 cm and perhaps in the LF cut -120 cm (ill. 5, 18). It doesn't seem to be too extended.

And there is a last site in the South to be seen in orange in the HF cut -100 cm and deeper and also in the LF cut -100 cm (ill. 16, 20,14).

When we talk about "sites" or even "wreck sites" this is to understand cum grano salis. The sonar is just telling, that there is a difference in the intensity of the signal. Looking at the surrounding, you may argue whether this difference is caused by natural phenomena or by "human interference", which we call an anomaly in the data. So you cannot tell exactly that there is a shipwreck or part of it or a contaminated site in Parker's sense, but you can only tell that there are anomalies and try to interpret them. But if ever there should be a project to do excavations in the outer area of the harbour these "sites" would be the places to begin with. There may be also other finding places in that area and certainly there are, but the highest concentration and hence the most promising operation is given in the "sites" indicated here.

There is still another puzzling situation: in the HF cut of -120 (ill. 20) you have a row of green dots in the actual "entrance" of the harbour leading to west like pearls on a string and bending at the end to north. The same is still to see also in the HF cut of -100cm (ill. 10) and once sensitised one may find it also in the other pictures, most impressively in the LF sum ups (ill. 7, 11,15,19).

This structure is about 120 m long in the western direction and about 60 m in the northern direction. The statement of the sonar signal is, that there are softer spots in a harder surrounding. In general this indicates sites or places where some hard material came to ly, caused a depression and went off. Why and when it went off is not to tell without further investigation. But anyway the depression was filled with soft sediment and the sonar detects it.

It is highly hazardous to dare an interpretation, but on the level of hypotheses one may assume a wooden or whatever substructure for a mole, protected from the South and open to the North. Following this idea we have the main entrance of the harbour in the South and a secondary entrance in the middle of the harbour facing north. Perhaps it was a sort of rescue entrance in case of strong winds or high seas from the South.

Appendix A

The harbour (inside area)

The harbour of Apollonia falls into three parts. This you can see by the sonar data and not in natura. In the south, where the entrance was, you have an area of about 50*50 m with a relatively dense concentration of material. This area is followed by a long part of the harbour, about 150 m, which is mostly empty. There are only some finding spots here and there. In the northern part, where the actual entrance is, you have again concentrations of finding spots mixed with rocks.

The concentration of material is obvious. Since the western entrance is actually in use, you should mainly expect recent material. At least near the surface of the bottom, the situation may change if we go deeper into the sediment.

Let us have a look to the anomalies mapped in the text illustration (note: the black lines bare no further information, they are just there for better orientation).

In the south we have this big area in

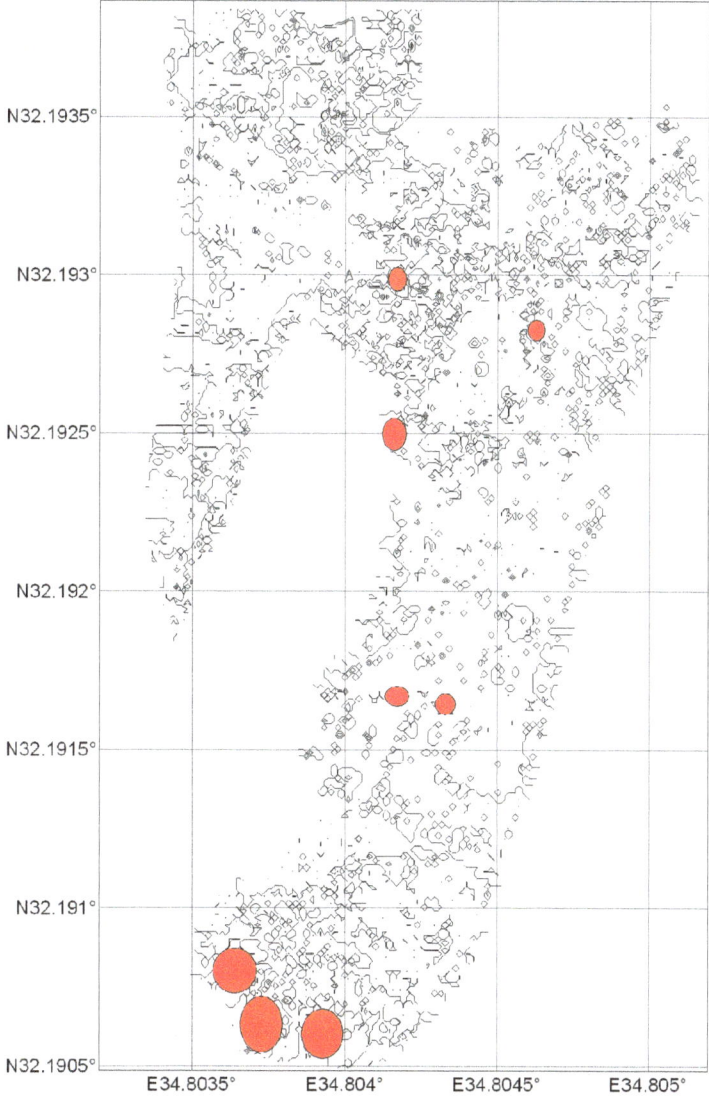

Indication of possible sites - inside area

75

orange in the HF sum up -20 cm (ill. 25), structured by 3 oblong areas in magenta. While the orange area diminishes, when we go deeper in the HF sum ups (ill. 29,33), the areas in magenta remain. This evokes the idea of material scattered over the bottom, while its concentration in the magenta areas is more dense. The scattered material may reach the depth of 40 cm in the sediment according to the HF cut -40 cm (ill. 28). You can see this situation also in the other pictures, especially well in the LF sum ups, but I avoid enumerating them all here. This area is highly promising and if it is not too disturbed by recent material, good results are to expect.

In the middle of the "empty corridor" there are two sites that deserve attention. The eastern one is to see in the HF sum up -20 cm as an orange spot (ill. 25) and it is to encounter again only in the HF cut -20 cm (ill. 24) and the LF cut -40 cm (ill. 26). It may be small, but it is too isolated to be neglected. The other one, western to it, is even harder to find. It is very small, but has some strong signals. It can be seen in the HF sum up -20 cm (ill. 25) as a very small orange dot, but then again in the LF cuts -20, -40, -100 and -120 cm (ill. 22,26,34,37).

When we leave the "empty corridor" and proceed to the area of the western entrance, we meet another site right in the southern corner of the entrance. The site seems to be covered on the surface by beach rock in the LF cut -20 cm (ill.22), but it develops to something else in the depth as seen in the HF cuts -20 cm and -100 cm (ill.24,36). The intensity of its signal is shown by the HF sum ups -20 cm, -40 cm and -80 cm (ill.25,29,33). It is visible in all LF sum ups.

Directly north to it and, so to say, in the middle of the entrance is situated another area of about 50 m of extension. It is best to find in the LF sum up -120 cm (ill.38), because there it shows as an isolated orange area in a yellow and blue surrounding. This area is present in all sum ups of LF and HF. In the HF cuts of -80 cm and -120 cm (ill.32,39) there are even black signals mixed within, that means very hard material.

One last spot deserves to be mentioned, lying eastern to the aforementioned site and in the middle of the harbour. It is only to see in the LF sum up -100 cm and -120 cm (ill.35,38). It is small and it has relatively weak signals, but could be an anomaly as well.

We have found no traces of wall in the harbour basin. In the area that we measured there was only water. We have found two areas of archaeological interest: the entrance area in the south and the entrance area in the West. It is by no way excluded that there is a lot more finding spots everywhere in the harbour. To study the southern area would be to my opinion a promising way to the understanding of the complexity of that harbour. Further considerations are not subject to this paper.

Dr. Hanz Günter Martin

Appendix A

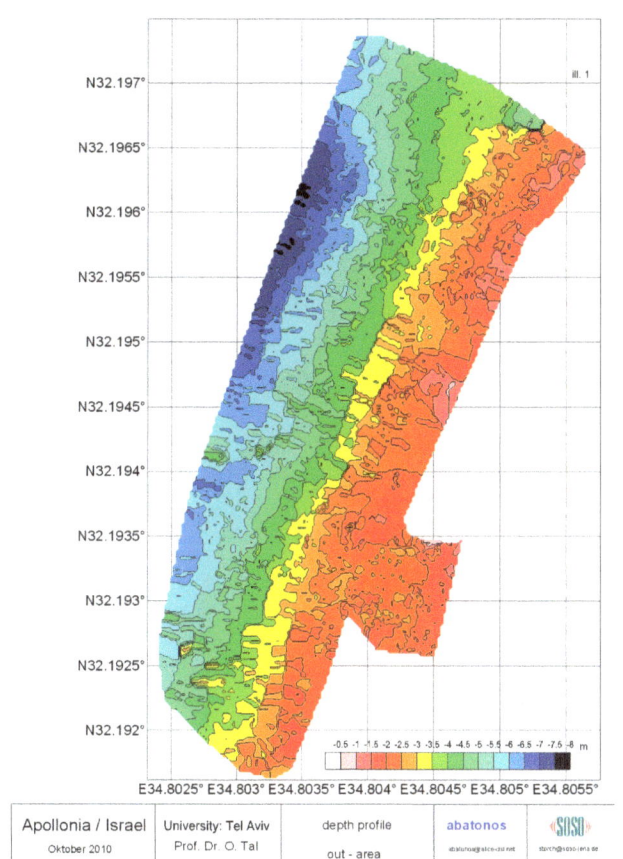
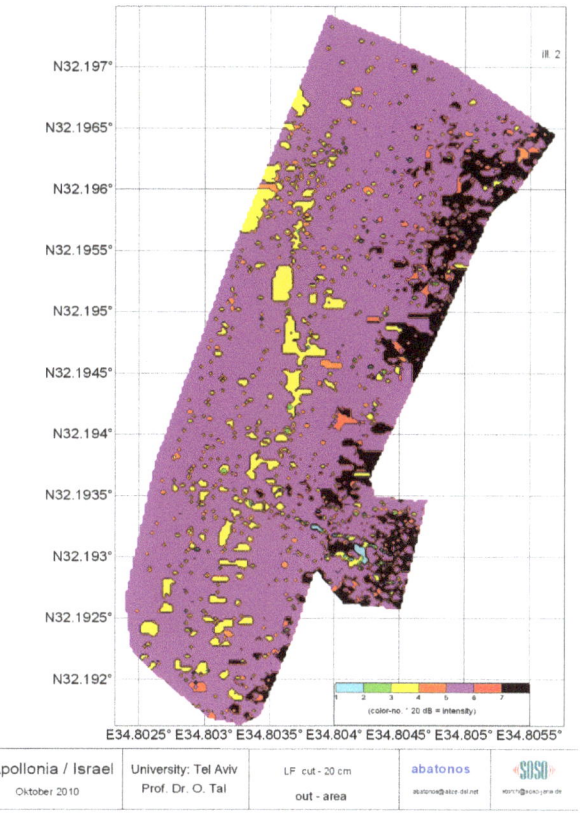
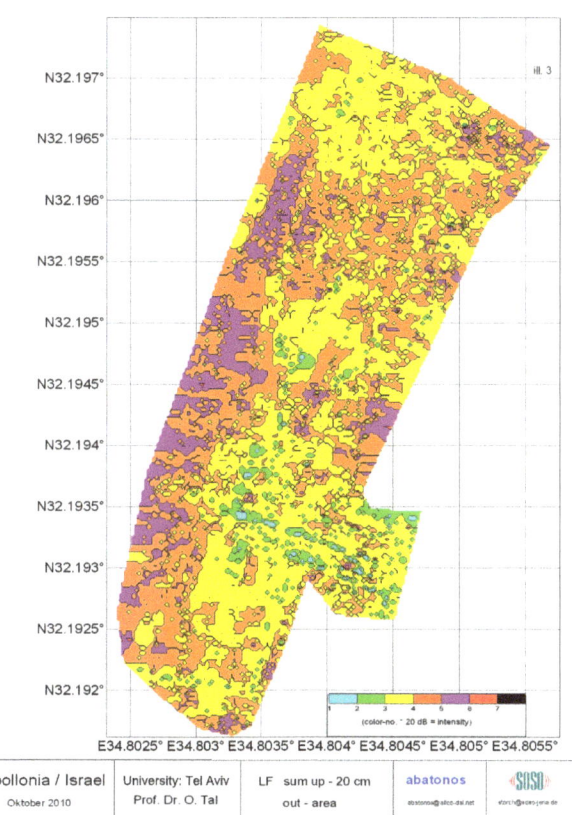
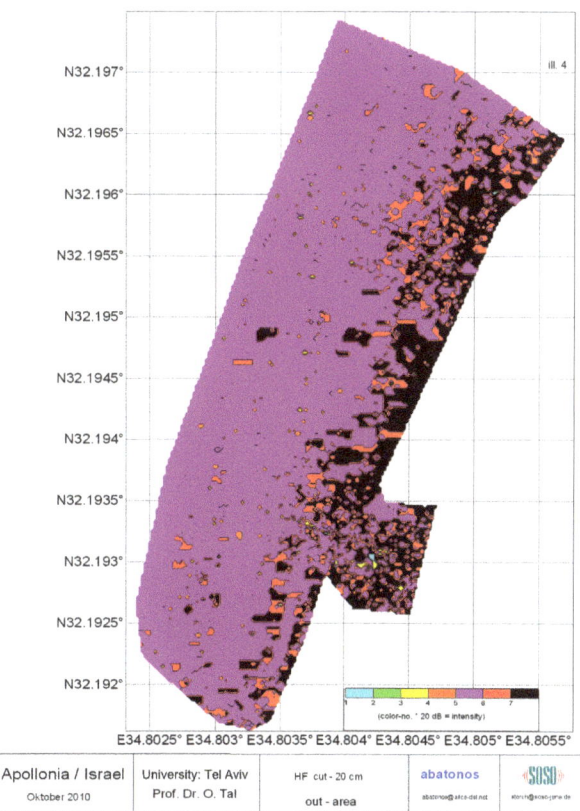

Sailing to the Holy Land

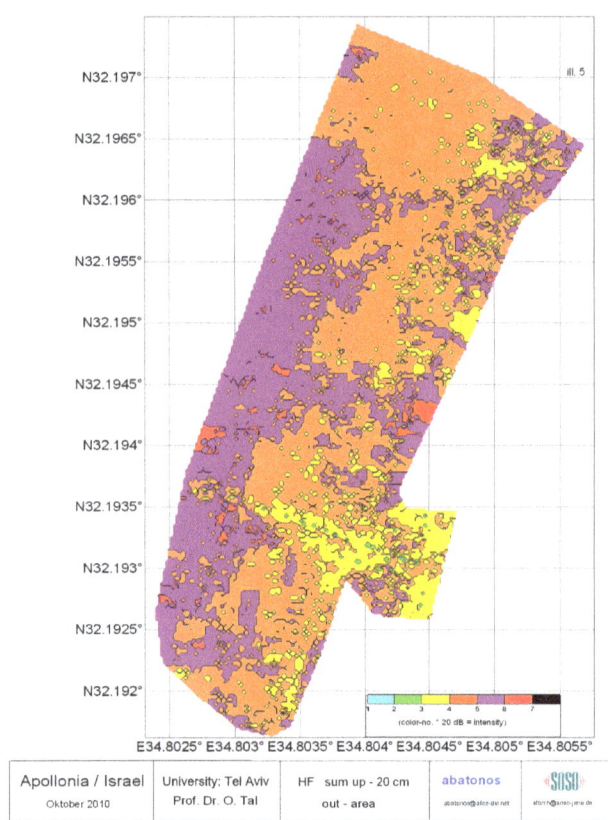
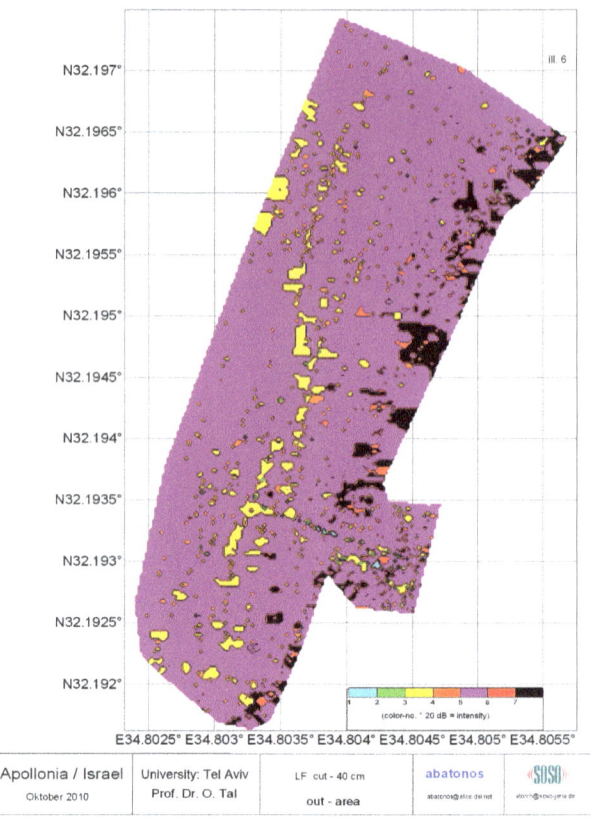
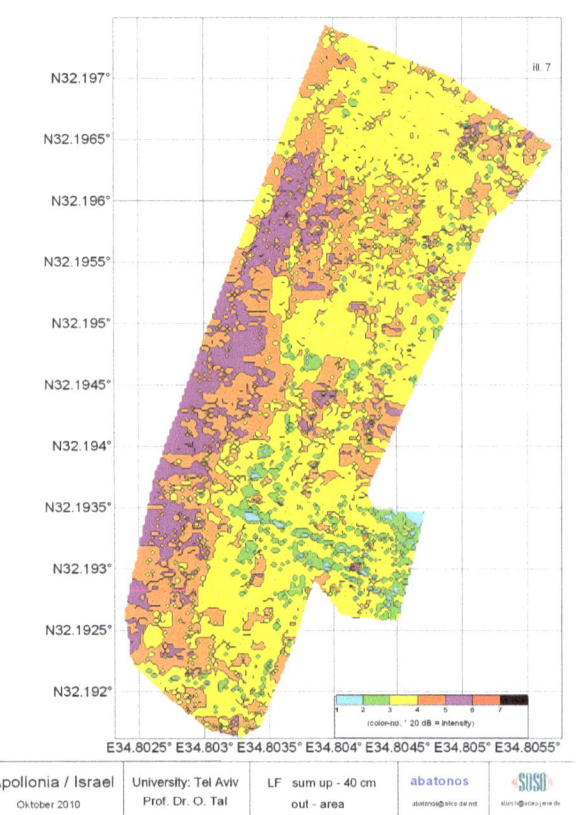
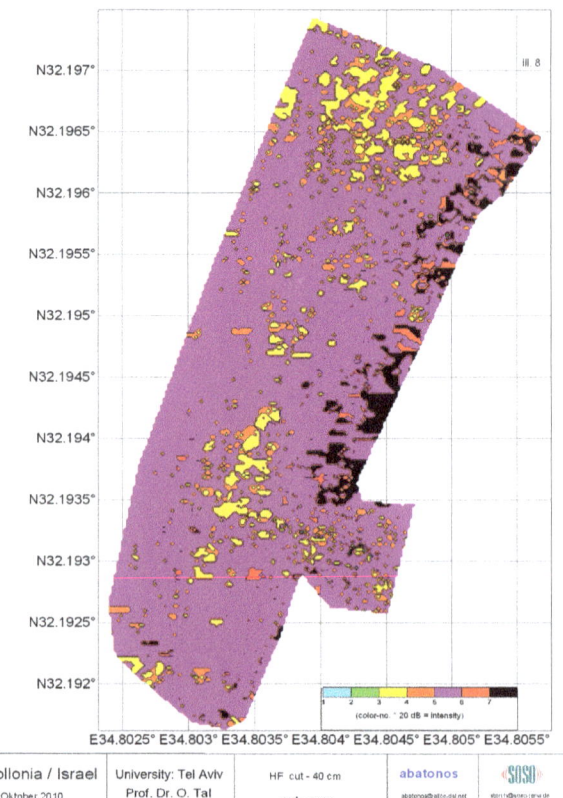

Appendix A

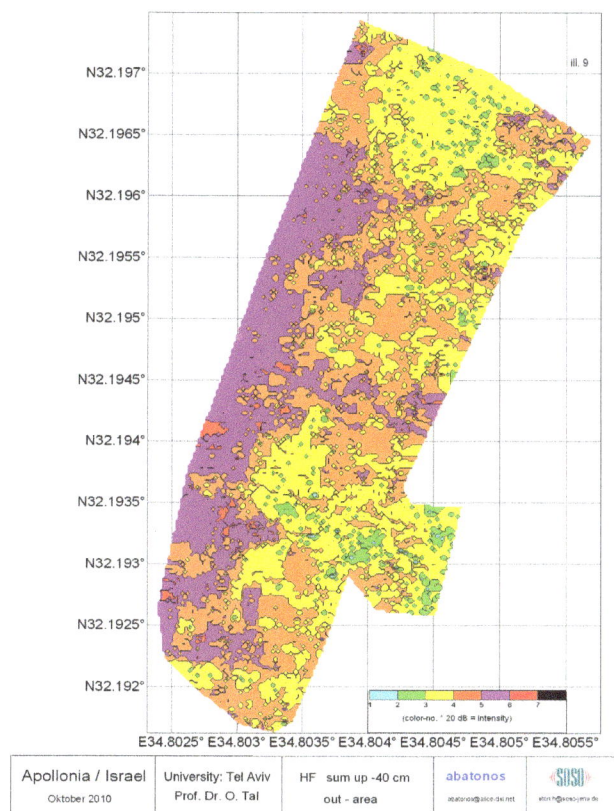

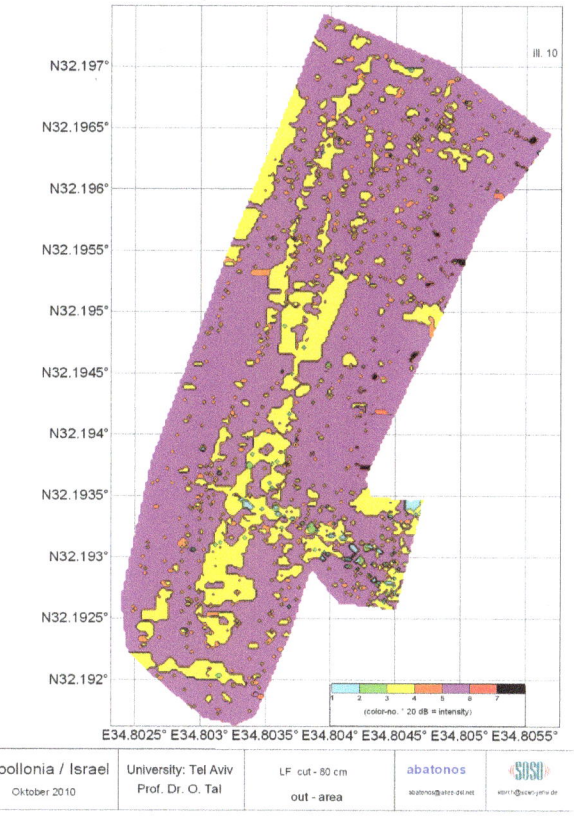

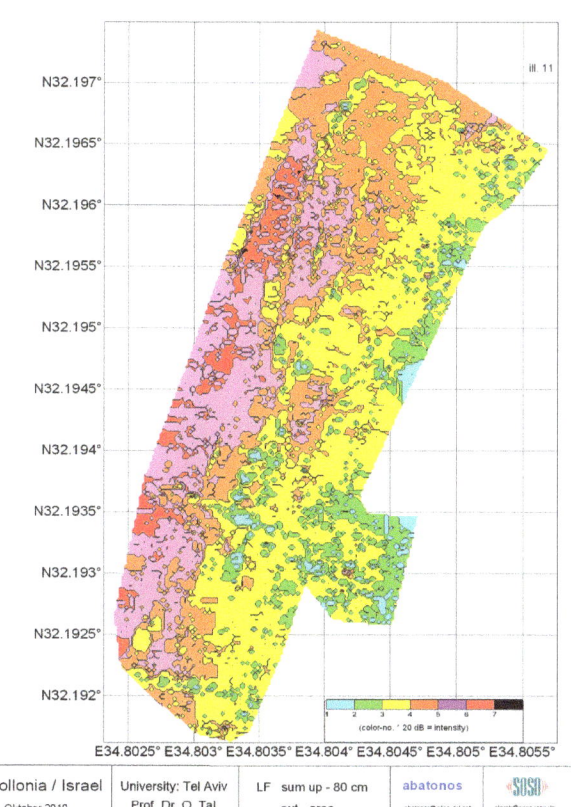

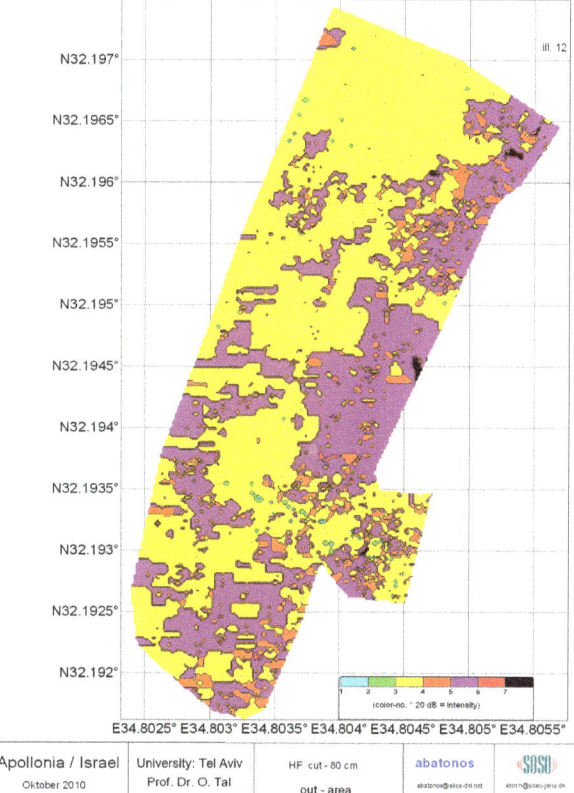

Sailing to the Holy Land

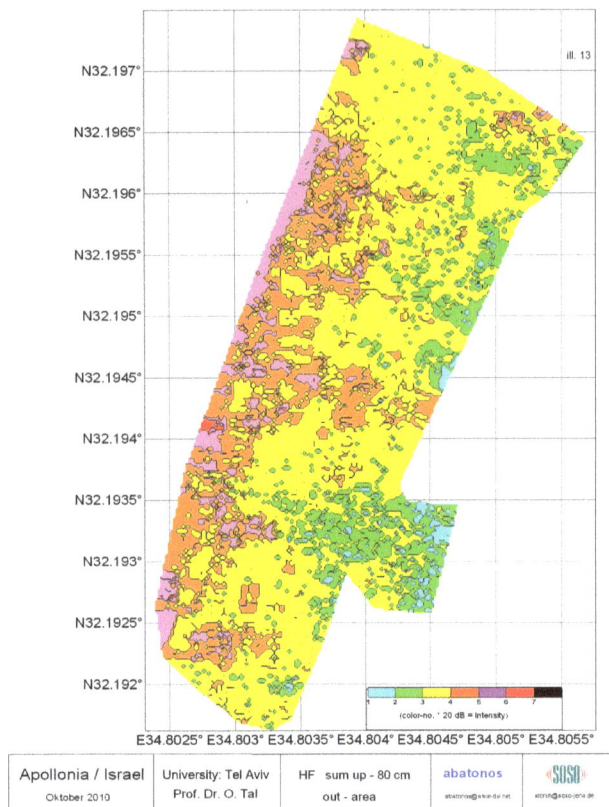
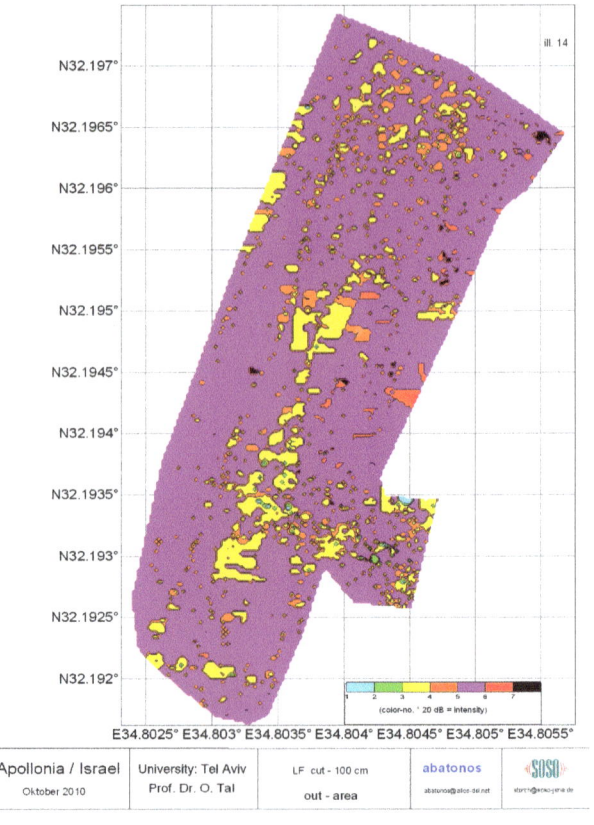
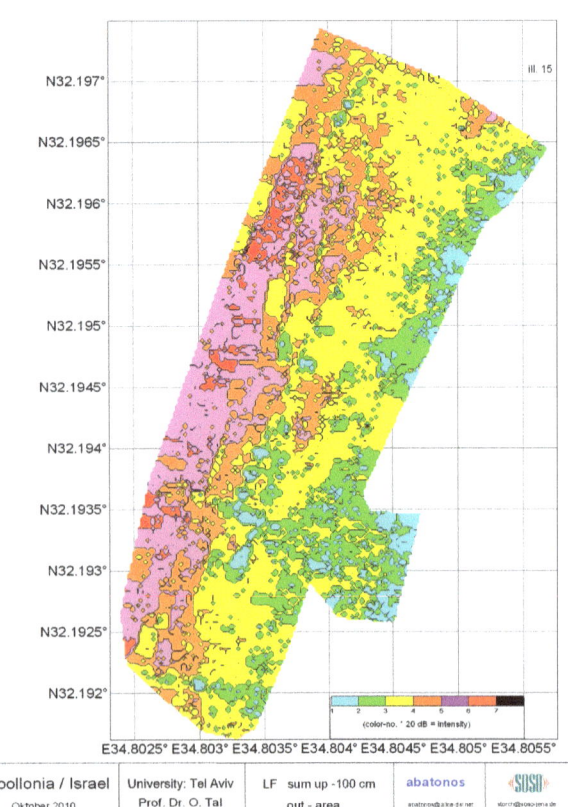
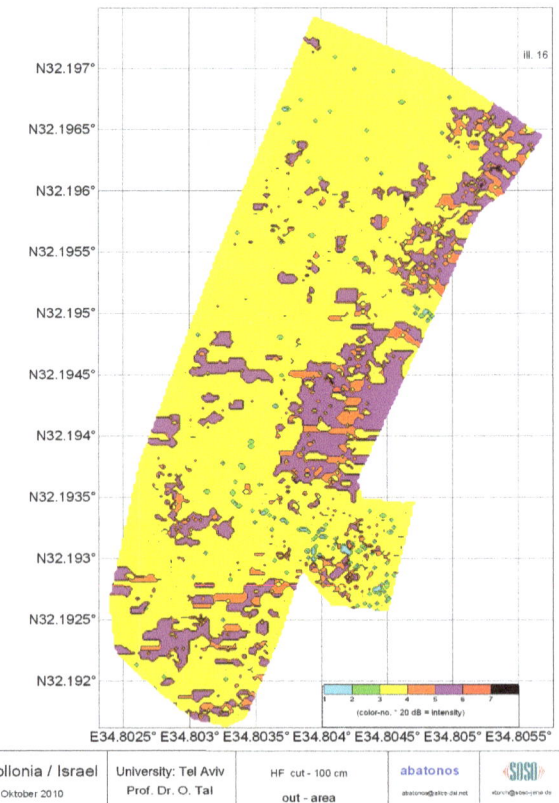

Appendix A

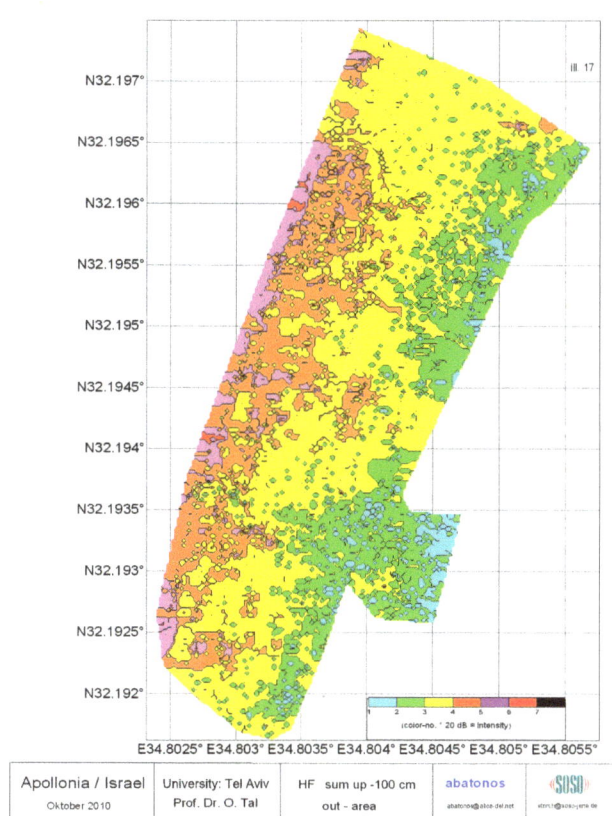
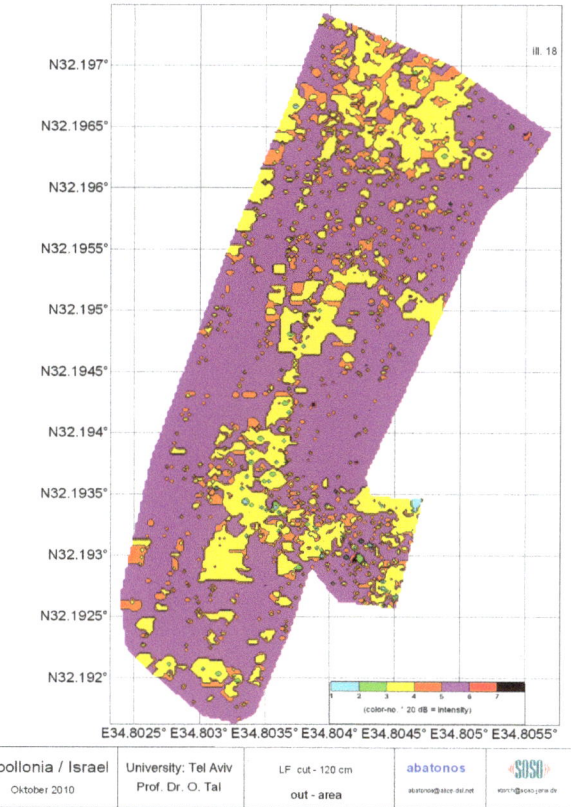
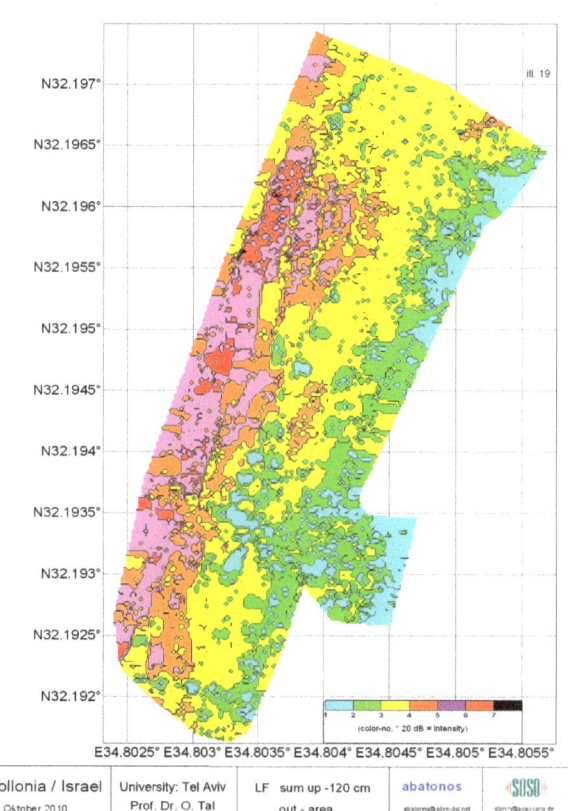
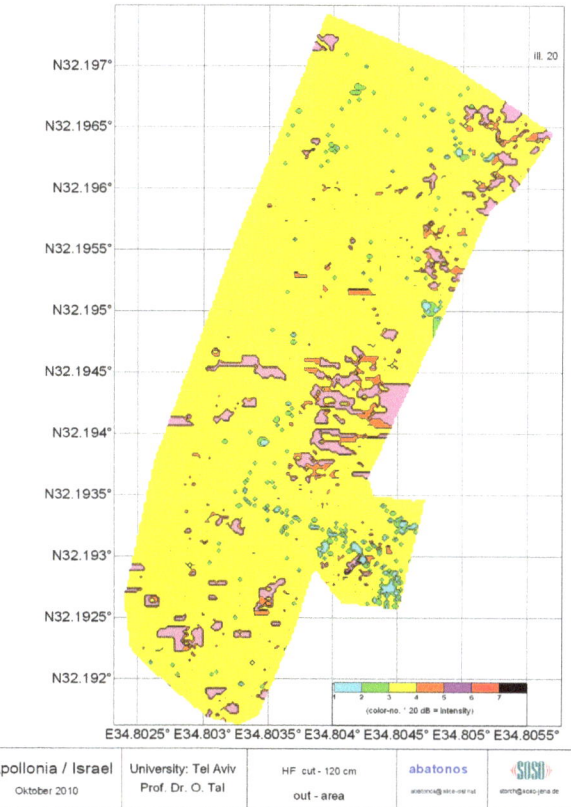

Sailing to the Holy Land

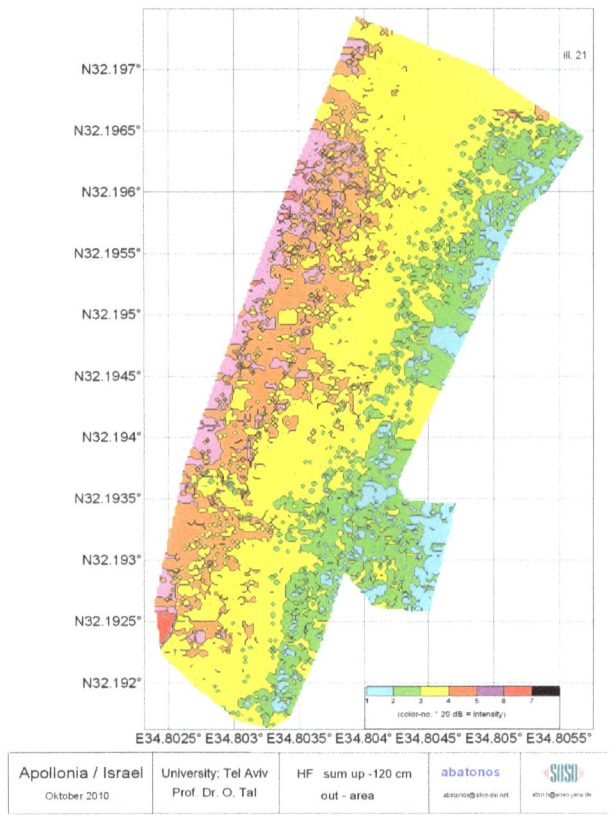
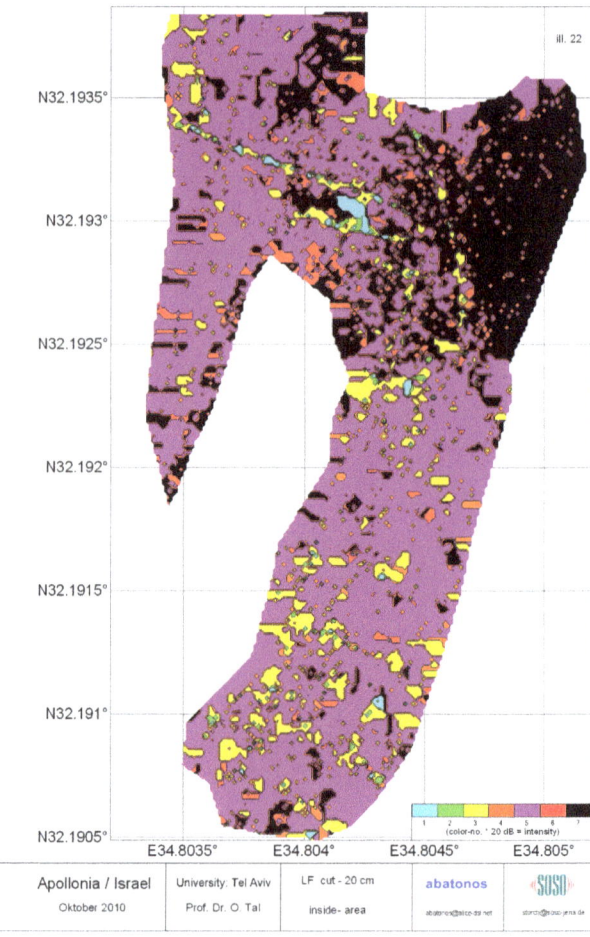
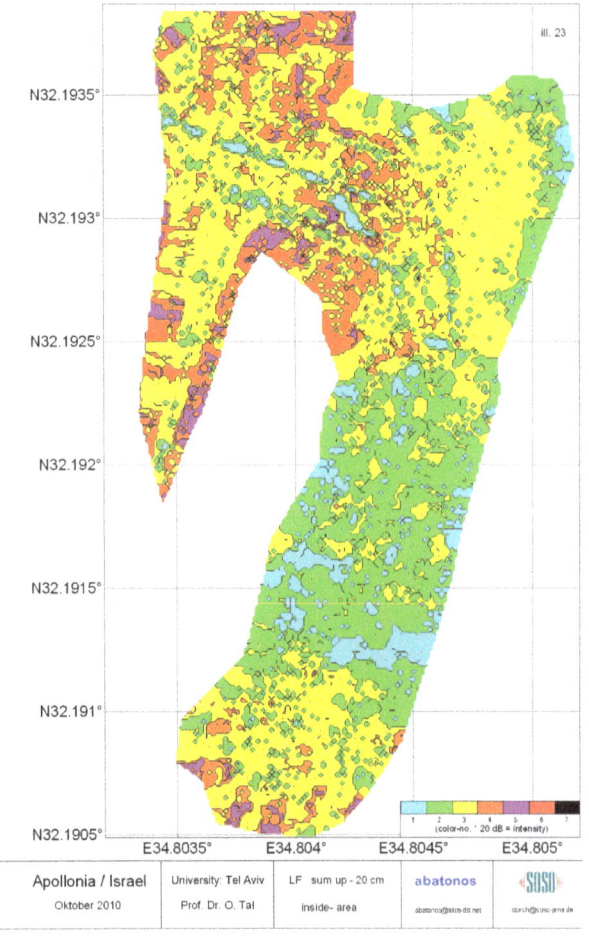
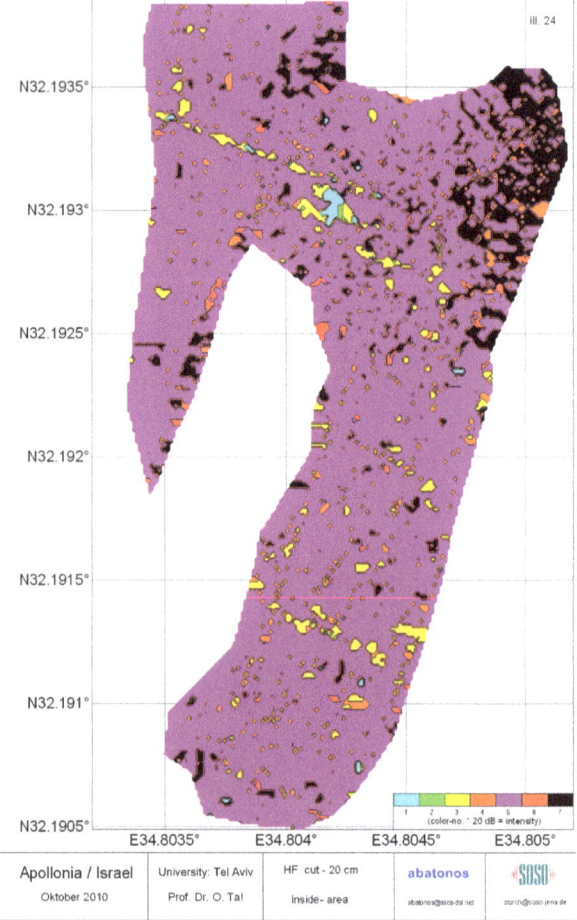

Appendix A

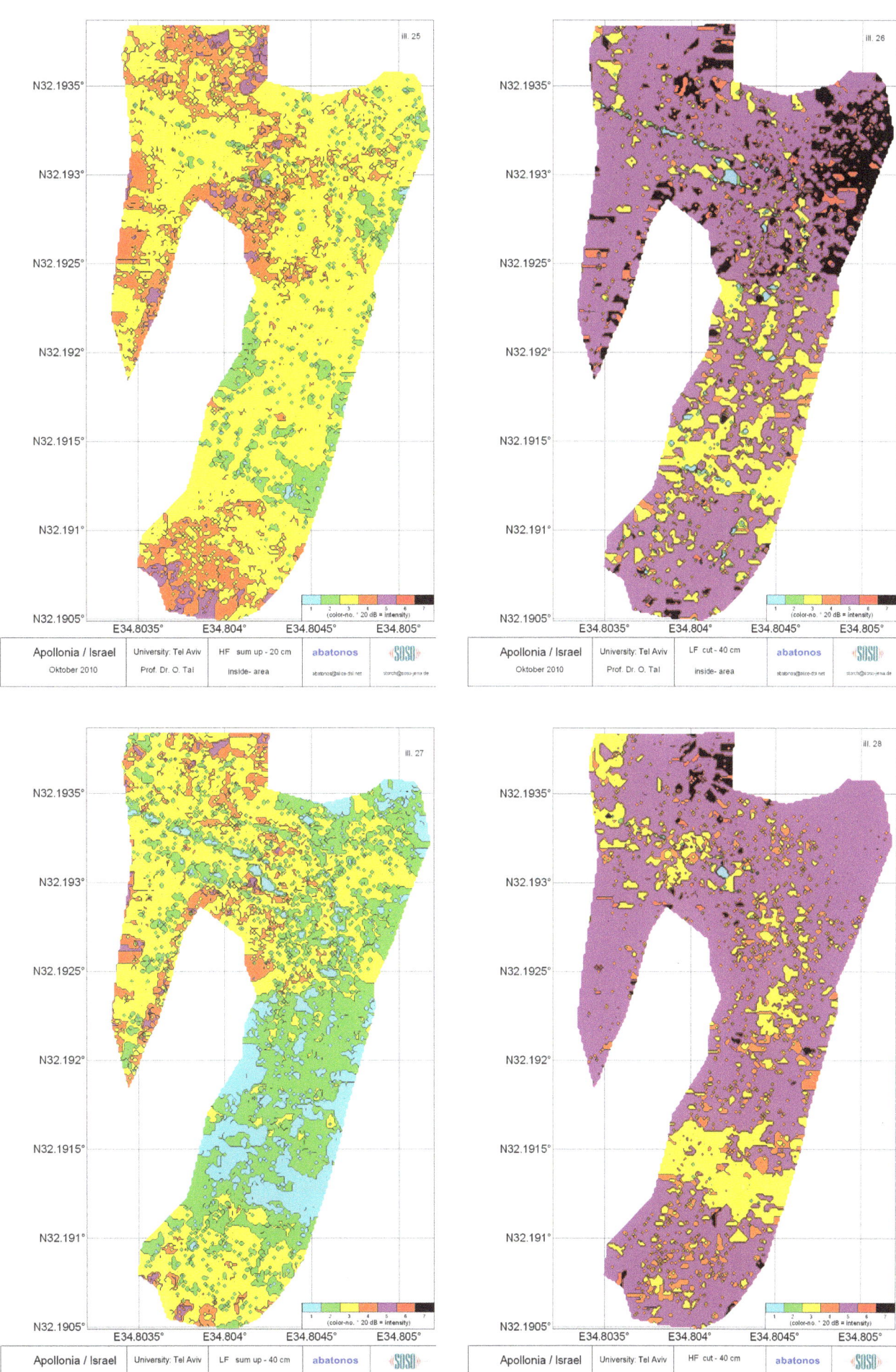

Sailing to the Holy Land

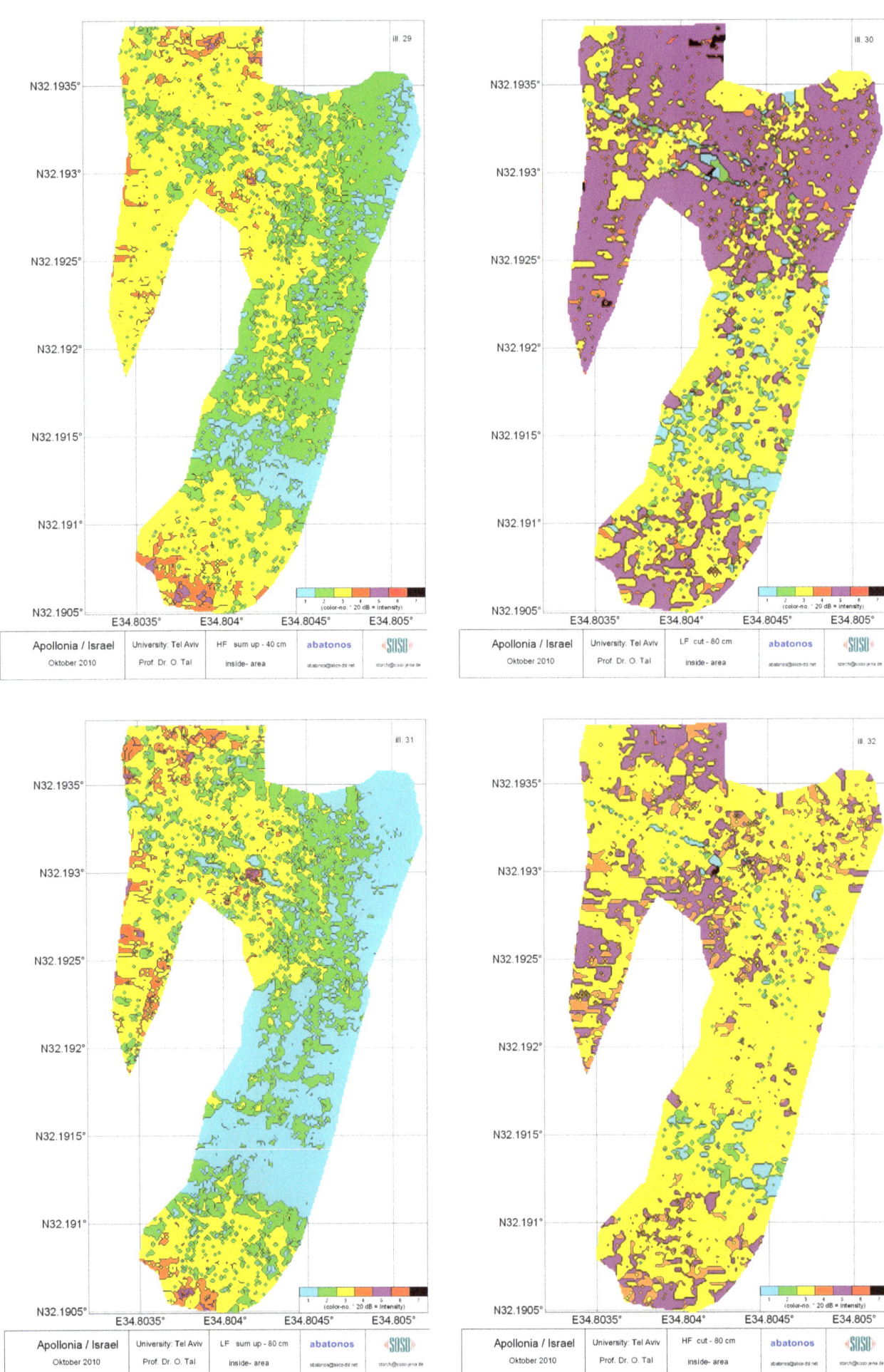

Appendix A

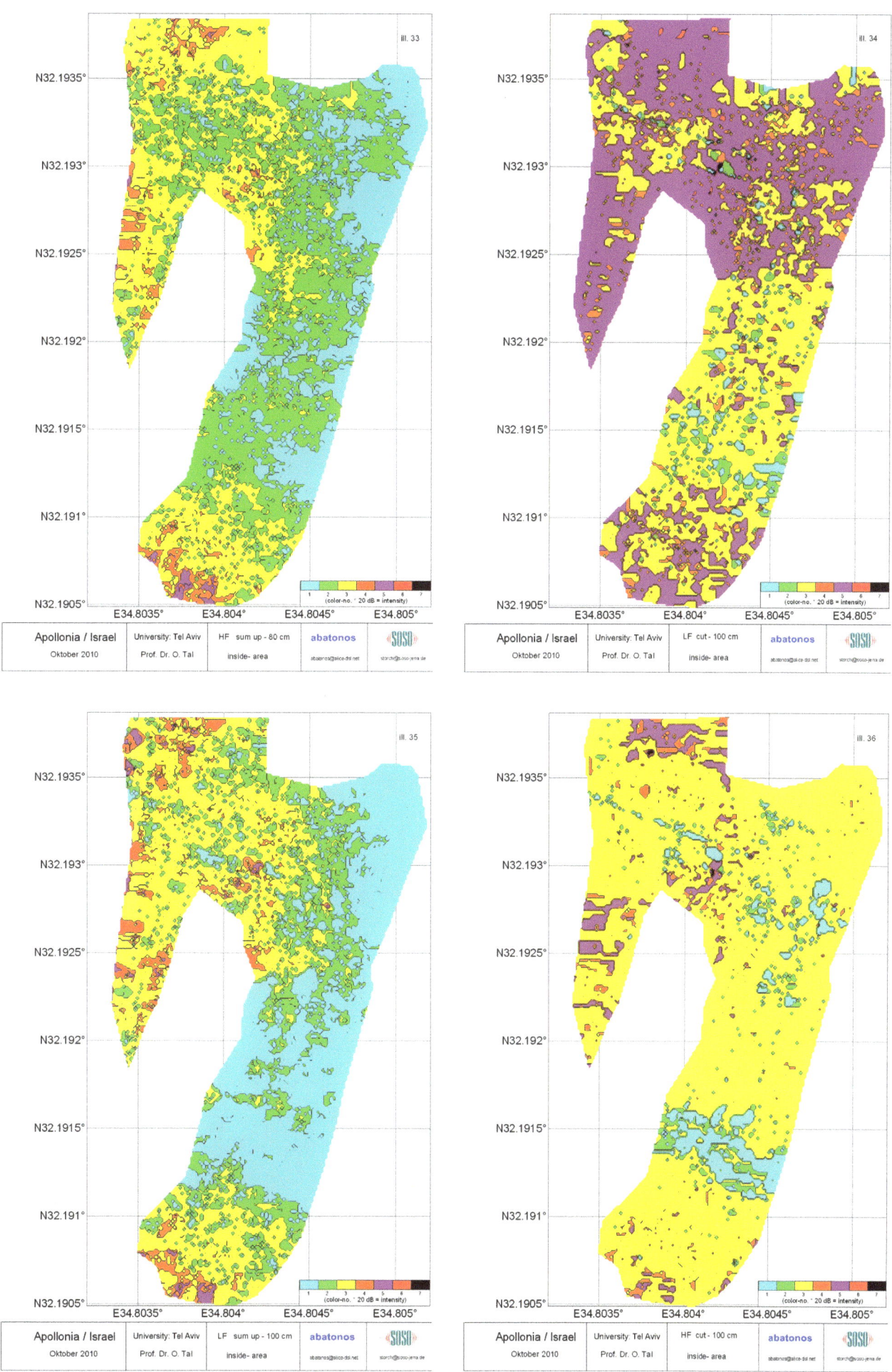

85

Sailing to the Holy Land

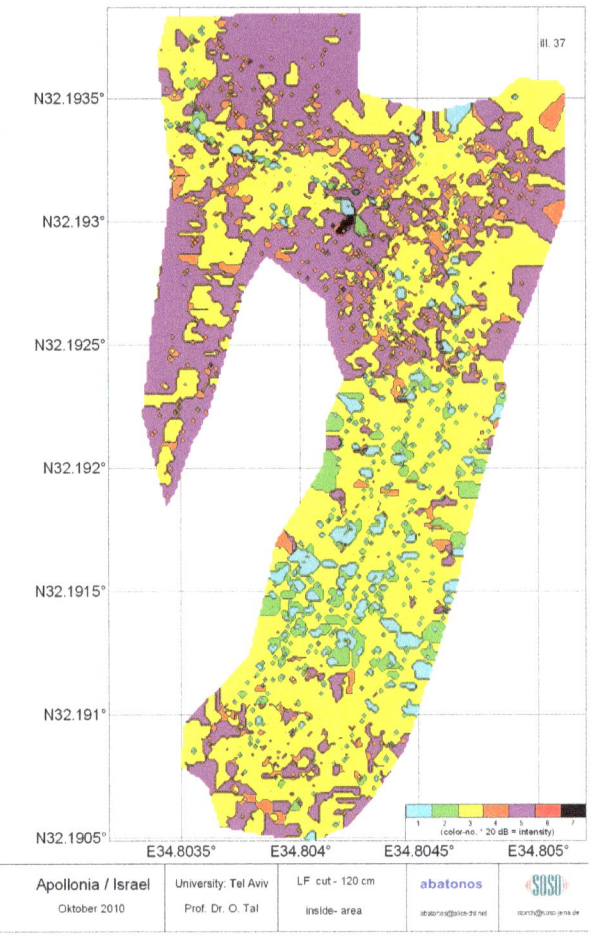
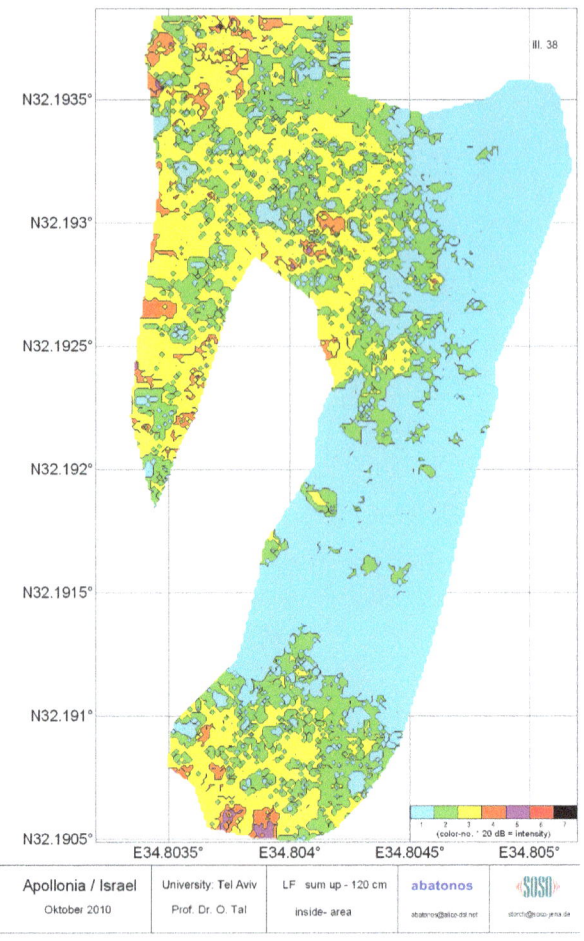
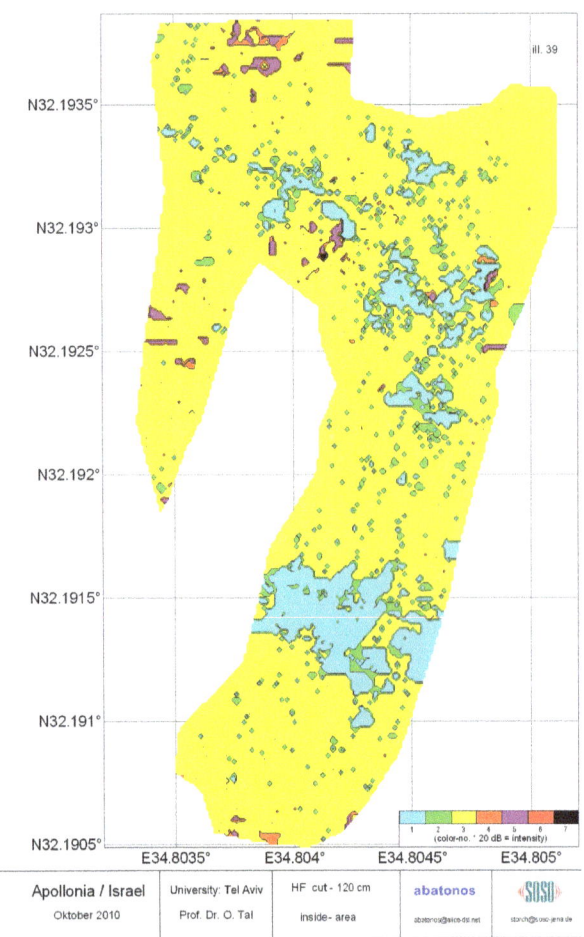

Appendix B

Positions of Targets Discovered by Sonar

Outer Area

1. 32° 11' 49.95" N;　34° 48' 13.9" E.
2. 32° 11' 49.5" N;　34° 48' 18.32" E.
3. 32° 11' 42.4" N;　34° 48' 13.5" E.
4. 32° 11' 40.0" N;　34° 48' 16.0" E.
5. 32° 11' 34.0" N;　34° 48' 12.2" E.

Inner Area

6. 32° 11' 6.0" N;　34° 48' 14.0" E.
7. 32° 11' 26.7" N;　34° 48' 13.5" E.
8. 32° 11' 26.13" N;　34° 48' 13.2" E.
9. 32° 11' 30.2" N;　34° 48' 13.9" E.
10. 32° 11' 29.8" N;　34° 48' 15.0" E.
11. 32° 11' 33.0" N;　34° 48' 14.7" E.
12. 32° 11' 34.8" N;　34° 48' 14.7" E.

Appendix C

List of Samples from Apollonia for Radiocarbon Dating Submitted to the AMS Lab
(Institut für Teilchenphysik Eidgenössische Technische Hochschule Hönggerberg, CH-8093 Zürich, Switzerland)
by Prof. Nili Liphschitz, Dan Mirkin and Prof. Oren Tal

Core	Sample Name and Number
1	New 3 – 3 – *
2	New 9 – 1 – *
2	New 9 – 3 A
2	New 9 – 4
2	New 9 – 5
2	New 9 – 7 A
2	New 9 – 7 C
3	New 10 – 1 – *
3	New 10 – 3 – *
3	New 10 – 4
3	New 10 – 5A
3	New 10 – 5C

* Results of these finds are shown starred in Table 2.

Appendix D

Equipment Transported to Expedition Camp by Boat

Angus Fire LD 1800 water-pump used for operating dredges and water-jetting.

Three sets of venturi dredgers, hoses, pipes, crates and one set of water-jetting equipment.

Plastic crates for transporting rubble and stones.

Fifteen sets of dive gear and diving suits.

Equipment for underwater documentation: drawing, recording and photography.

Measuring equipment.

Office supplies and dive log.

Camp equipment: tent, table, kitchenware.

Miscellaneous tools and equipment.

Supply motor boat and rubber boat.

Appendix E

Locations of Water-jetting in the 'Port' (redrawn by Ms. Michal Semo-Kovetz after original)

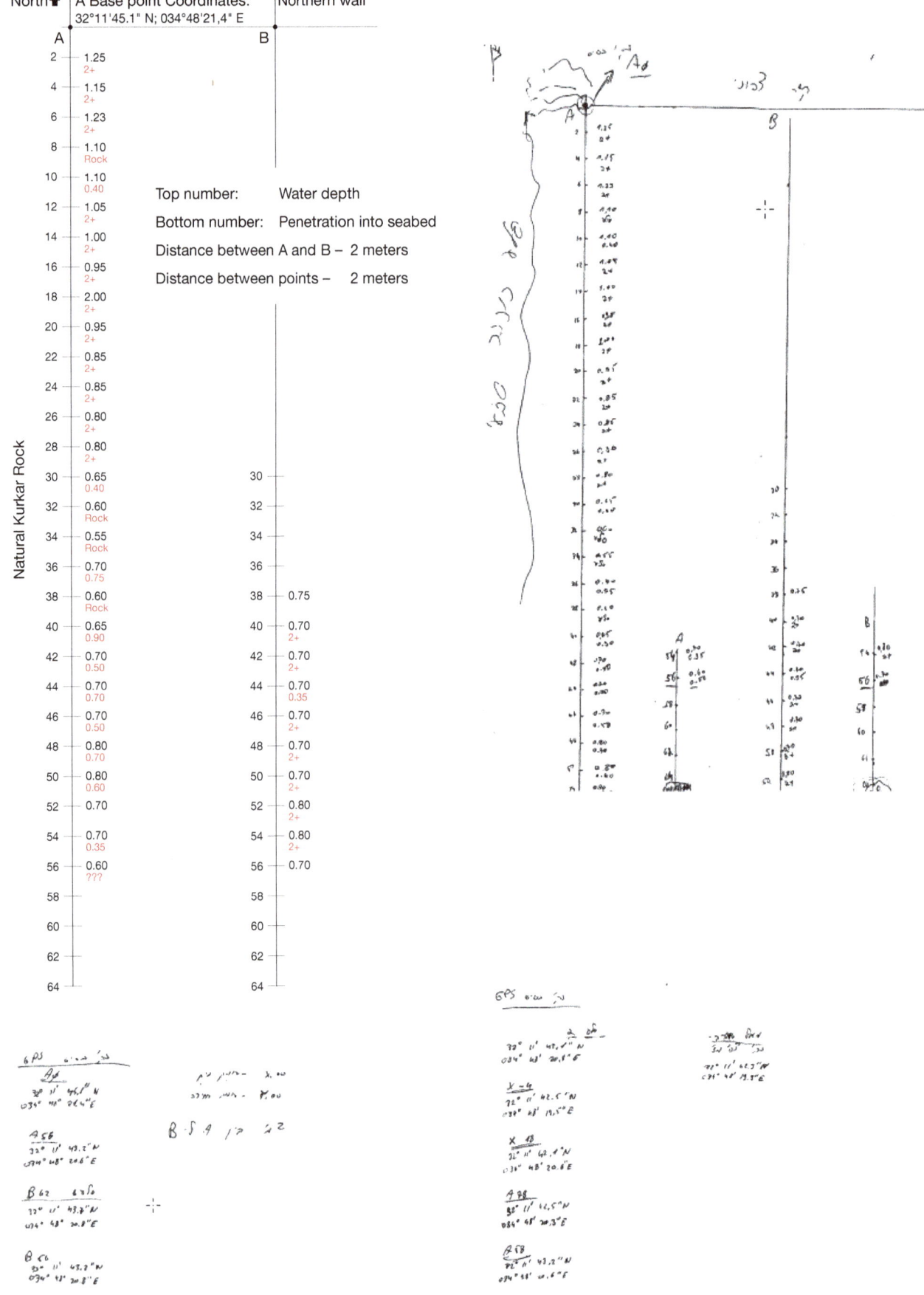

North ↑ | A Base point Coordinates: 32°11'45.1" N; 034°48'21,4" E | Northern wall

Top number: Water depth
Bottom number: Penetration into seabed
Distance between A and B – 2 meters
Distance between points – 2 meters

A		B	
2	1.25 / 2+		
4	1.15 / 2+		
6	1.23 / 2+		
8	1.10 / Rock		
10	1.10 / 0.40		
12	1.05 / 2+		
14	1.00 / 2+		
16	0.95 / 2+		
18	2.00 / 2+		
20	0.95 / 2+		
22	0.85 / 2+		
24	0.85 / 2+		
26	0.80 / 2+		
28	0.80 / 2+		
30	0.65 / 0.40	30	
32	0.60 / Rock	32	
34	0.55 / Rock	34	
36	0.70 / 0.75	36	
38	0.60 / Rock	38	0.75
40	0.65 / 0.90	40	0.70 / 2+
42	0.70 / 0.50	42	0.70 / 2+
44	0.70 / 0.70	44	0.70 / 0.35
46	0.70 / 0.50	46	0.70 / 2+
48	0.80 / 0.70	48	0.70 / 2+
50	0.80 / 0.60	50	0.70 / 2+
52	0.70	52	0.80 / 2+
54	0.70 / 0.35	54	0.80 / 2+
56	0.60 / ???	56	0.70
58		58	
60		60	
62		62	
64		64	

Natural Kurkar Rock

Appendix E

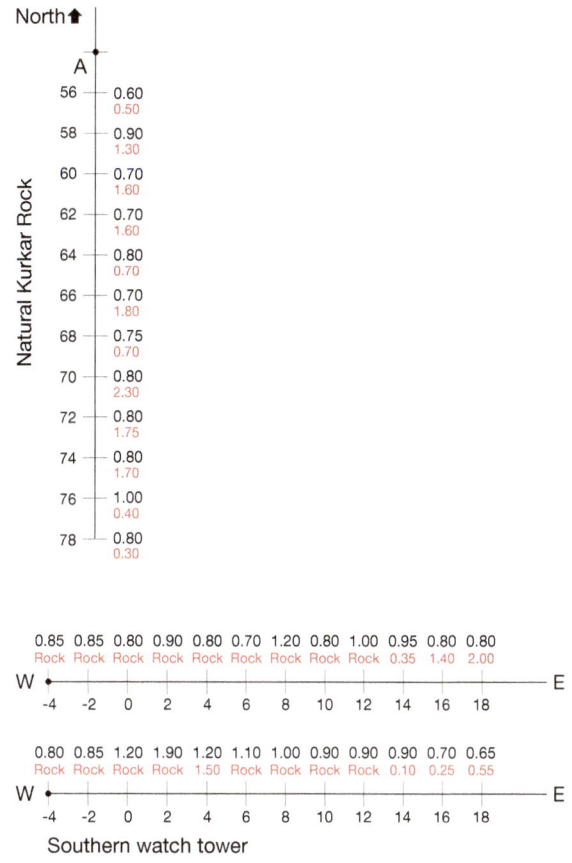

Southern wall

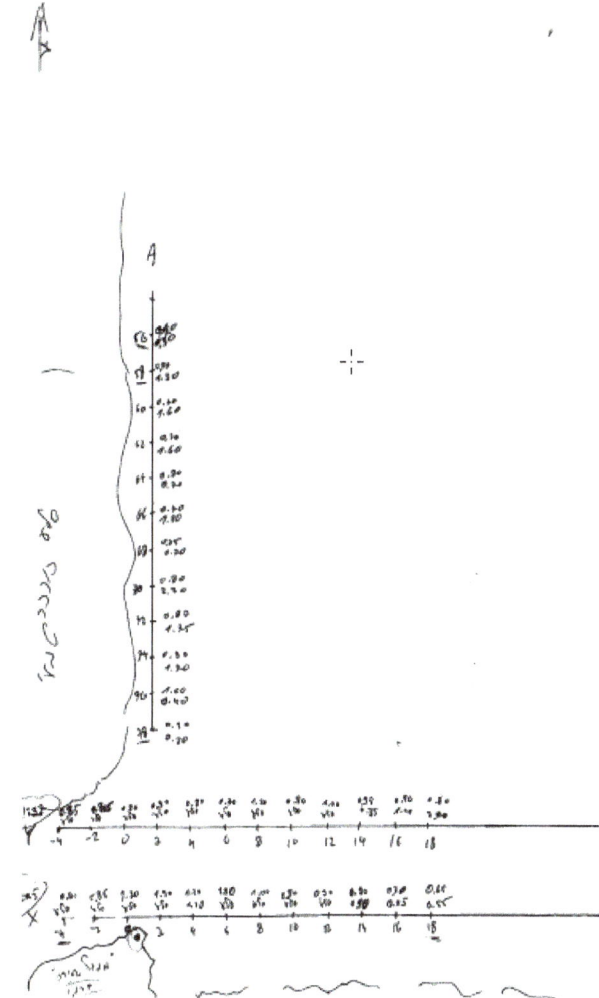

Appendix F

Original Underwater Drawing of the Western Part of the Northern Wall (J. B. Tresman)

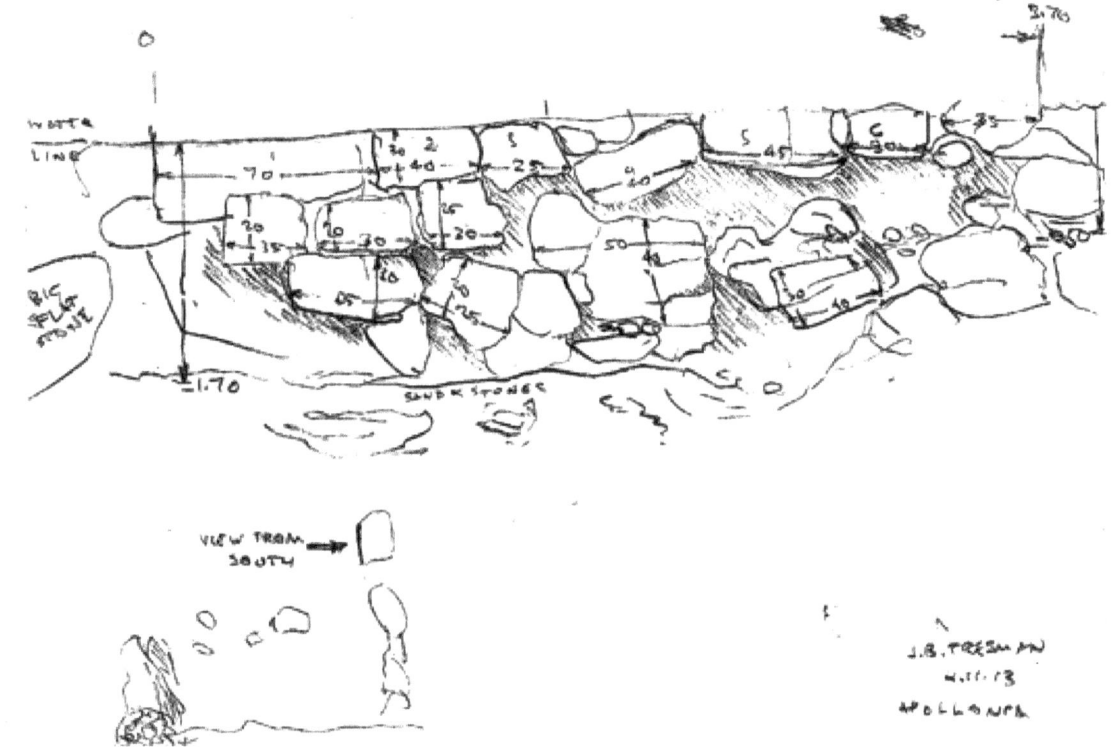

Appendix G

Tide Table for 6 November 2013

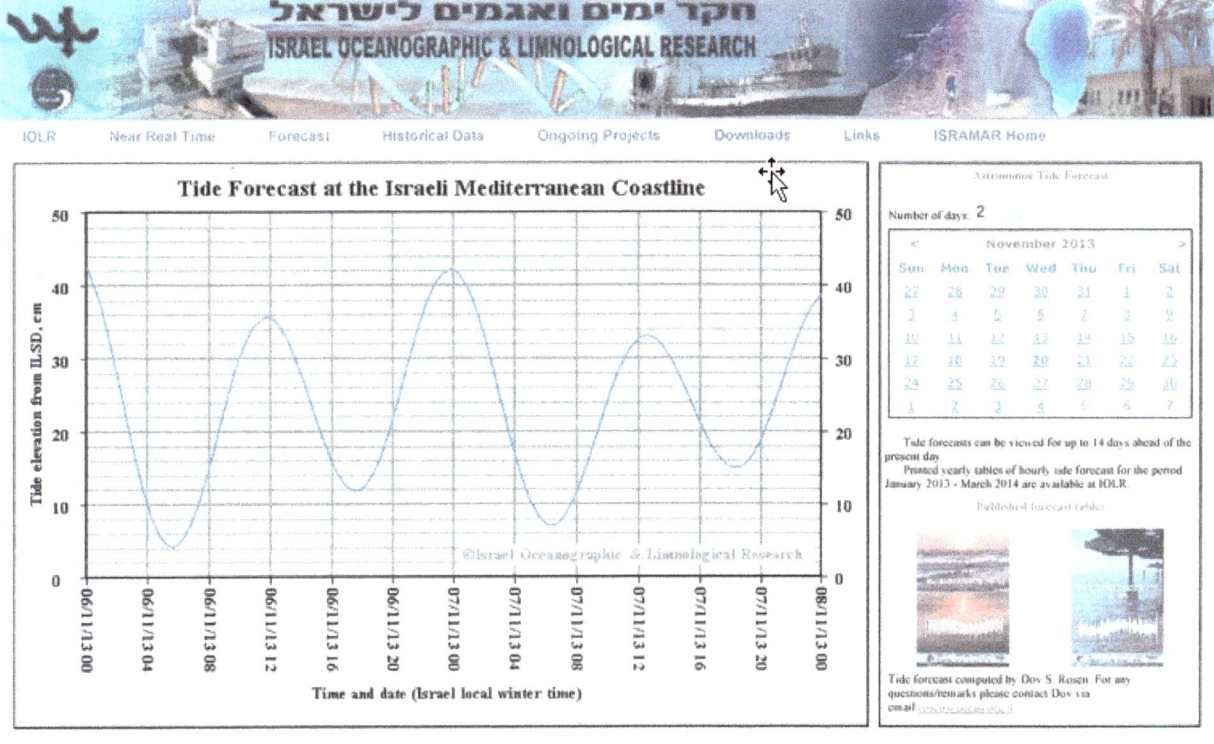

Appendix H

GIS Representation of the Apollonia Installation

The bold black line signifies the western sew wall – the natural reef.

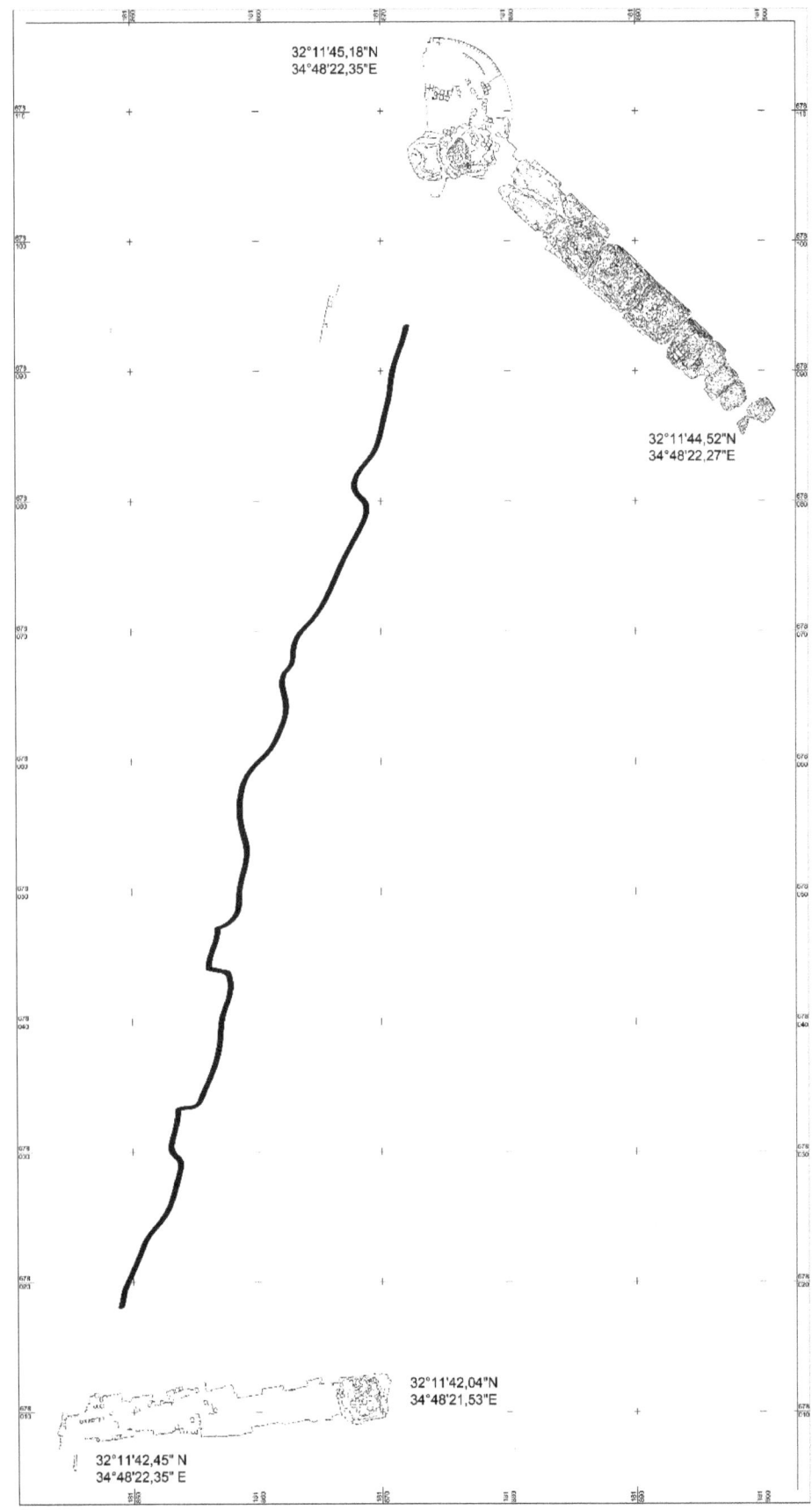

Appendix I

Excerpts from Ambroise – L'estoire de la Guerre Sainte, in Old French

Arrival of messengers from Jaffa:

Le seir al vespre, en teie atente,
Elh vos une barge abrivee
Venir a Acre e arivee;
E cil qui de la barge eissirent
Vindrenl al rei, plus n'atendirent.
Si lui distrent que Jaffe iert prise,
E la gent al Thoron assise,
S'ele n'iert par lui sucorue.
Que tote iert morte e encorue.
Si come jo vos ai conté;
E li preuz reis par sa bonté'
Leissa tôt son porposement
E dist : "Joi irai veirement".
(Ambroise 10958 – 10970)

Richard prays for good wind in Haifa

Devers la mer d'un vent contraire
Noz autres genz sunt deslorbees,
E li rois e ces des gualees,
Si que detreis jorz ne se murent
De soz Chaiphas ou il jurent,
E que li reis diseit : " Merci,
"Deu! por quoi me tenez ici?
Ja vois eu vostre servise!"
Mais Danipnedeus par sa franchise
Lor envoia un vent de boire,
  (Ambroise 11016-11025)

King Richard landing in Jaffa

Lors fist traire avant ses galees;
Ses jambes totes désarmées
Sailli des ci qu'a la çainture
En mer"o sa bone aventure
E vint a force a tere sesche
Secont ou prims, ço fu sa teche.